Parish Councils: Pastoral and Finance

By James A. Coriden and Mark F. Fischer

CLSA Pastoral Resources

© Copyright 2016 by the Canon Law Society of America

ISBN: 978-1-932208-43-6
SAN: 237-6296

The Canon Law Society of America's programs and publications are designed solely to help canonists maintain their professional competence. In dealing with specific canonical matters, the canonist using Canon Law Society of America (CLSA) publications or orally conveyed information should also research original sources of authority.

The views and opinions expressed in this publication are those of the individual authors and do not represent the views of the CLSA, its Board of Governors, staff or members. The CLSA does not endorse the views or opinions expressed by the individual authors. The publisher and authors specifically disclaim any liability, loss or risk, personal or otherwise, which is incurred as consequence, directly or indirectly, of the use, reliance, or application of any of the contents of this publication.

Unless otherwise noted, all canons quoted are from the *Code of Canon Law, Latin-English Edition* (Washington, DC: Canon Law Society of America, 2012) and the *Code of Canons of the Eastern Churches, Latin-English Edition* (Washington, DC: Canon Law Society of America, 2002).

Printed in the United States of America.

Canon Law Society of America
Office of the Executive Coordinator
415 Michigan Avenue Northeast
Suite 101
Washington, DC 20017-4502

Contents

Introduction 1

PART ONE: *Parish Pastoral Councils*

1: Theological Framework for Pastoral Councils 5
2: Canonical Framework for Pastoral Councils 10
3: Roots in the Second Vatican Council and Subsequent
   Documents 14
4: Functions of the Parish Pastoral Council 19
5: Parish Pastoral Council Relationships 25
6: Membership in the Parish Pastoral Council 31
7: Operation of the Parish Pastoral Council 37
8: The Process for Pastoral Planning 44

PART TWO: *Parish Finance Councils*

9: Theological Framework for Finance Councils 53
10: Canonical Framework for Finance Councils 59
11: Roots in the Second Vatican Council and Other
    Documents 63
12: Functions of the Parish Finance Council 67
13: Parish Finance Council Relationships 73
14: Membership in the Parish Finance Council 79
15: Operation of the Parish Finance Council 82
Conclusion: Consultation as Collaboration 91

Sources 95

CONTENTS

Introduction

PART ONE: Pastoral Councils

1. Theological Framework for Pastoral Councils
2. The Right Frame for the Pastoral Council
3. Setting up the Parish Pastoral Council and Subsequent Documentation
4. Functions of the Parish Pastoral Council
5. Parish Registers' Correct Establishing
6. Membership of the Parish Pastoral Council
7. Committees of the Parish Pastoral Council
8. The Process for Pastoral Planning

PART TWO: Parish Finance Councils

9. Theological Framework: The Finance Council
10. The role of Finance and Parish Finance Council
11. Setting up of the Parish Finance Council and Other Documentation
12. Functioning of the Parish Finance Council
13. Parish Finance Council Relationships
14. Membership of the Parish Finance Council
15. Operation of the Parish Finance Council
16. Concept of Cooperation & Collaboration

Conclusion

Introduction

The dynamics of parish life in the United States have changed greatly since the close of the Second Vatican Council fifty years ago. One factor that changed the dynamics was the Council's emphasis on the active participation of the laity in the life of the Church. Another was the recommendation that pastors consult their parishioners in various matters of concern to the parish. This book examines consultation through parish councils, both pastoral and financial. Vatican II laid the groundwork for such councils in the hope that their members might offer prudent advice and that pastors might make wiser decisions after listening to them.

This book describes the nature and operation of the two councils. With their roots in Vatican II, these councils offer parishioners a share in the pastoral and administrative responsibilities of their pastors. They also allow the pastors and their parishes to benefit from the practical wisdom and experience of their people. Pastors and their parishioners are co-responsible for the well-being of their parish community, each according to the gifts and insights the Holy Spirit has given them.

The book is intended for the use of those who care about the life of their parish, but especially parishioners who are members of one of the councils, or are considering such membership, parish staff members, and, of course, pastors. It offers an in-depth vision of the origins and development of the councils, including the theological and canonical reasoning behind them. It also describes their functions, operations, and relationships to other elements of the parish, such as the parish staff, and other committees and organizations, as well as the pastor.

This book draws upon a variety of resources, many of which are noted in the text and in the list of sources at the end of the book: theological teachings, canonical documents, survey research, and the books and articles of scholars.

In addition, the book attempts to draw out what is implicit in the church's official documents, namely, a theology of ecclesial consultation and the relationship between pastor and parishioners.

Pastoral and finance councils provide a means for the pastor to collaborate constructively with his parishioners. The pastor knows his own role and gifts, and one of his challenges is to recognize and appreciate the talents and gifts of others. He gathers thoughtful people together and invites them to reflect with him about how to improve the parish in the pursuit of its mission. The pastor and his parishioners are mutually interdependent.

One of the pastor's tasks is to build the parish community, as the *Code of Canon Law* puts it, to help the faithful to care about, participate in, and promote the parish communion (c. 529 §2). He is to help them be "one in Christ." His leadership of, and their participation in, the celebration of the Eucharist is the culmination of that good work, the crowning symbol of their mutual collaboration in promoting communion. Communion is the unity and graced vitality that bonds the members of the parish community together.

Communion is primarily the work of the Holy Spirit. The authors of this book pray that the parish pastoral and finance councils will serve as apt instruments of the Holy Spirit of God in fostering parish communion.

This book was undertaken at the request of the Publications Advisory Board of the Canon Law Society of America. The authors edited the chapters together after James Coriden drafted chapters 1-3, 9-11 and 14, and Mark Fischer drafted chapters 4-8, 12-13 and 15.

July 2015

PART ONE:
PARISH PASTORAL COUNCILS

1: THEOLOGICAL FRAMEWORK FOR PASTORAL COUNCILS

Parishes benefit from the wisdom and deliberations of gifted parishioners, especially when pastors consult them in the form of a parish pastoral council. Catholics believe that the parish actualizes the Church of Christ in its own locale, that the pastor and parishioners collaborate in guiding it, and that wise counsel is a gift of God's Holy Spirit. This chapter explores the theological foundations underlying these beliefs about ecclesial consultation.

The Parish as Local Church

The parish is the very embodiment of the Church in a locality. The parish not only *represents* the Church universal in its own neighborhood, it *is* fully the Church. The Church is actualized, made real and alive, in the local parish. The parish is not like a local franchise or branch office of a huge corporation – like those of banks, or gas stations, or fast food shops. The parish makes the Church fully present, it completely embodies the Church, while maintaining close communion with the diocese and its bishop and with the Church universal and its pope, the Bishop of Rome.

The Second Vatican Council, in its *Dogmatic Constitution on the Church* (1965) spoke of the parish in these terms:

> The church of Christ is truly present in all the lawful local congregations of the faithful which, united with their pastors, are themselves called churches in the New Testament. For in their own locality, these are the new people called by God, in the Holy Spirit and with full conviction (1 Thes 1:5). In them the faithful are gathered together by the preaching of the gospel of Christ, and the mystery of the Lord's supper is celebrated . . . In these communities . . . Christ is present by whose power the one, holy, catholic and apostolic church is gathered together (n. 26).

Some years after the Council the *Code of Canon Law* (1983) enacted a complete set of regulations governing parishes and the ministries within them (cc. 515-552). In doing so, the Code defined parishes in terms of communities: "A parish is a certain community of the Christian faithful stably constituted in a particular church (i.e., a diocese), whose pastoral care is entrusted to a pastor ... under the authority of the diocesan bishop." The local community of faithful Catholic people is the heart of the matter.

As a general rule parishes are "territorial," that is their community includes all the Christian faithful within given geographical boundaries, but they can also be "personal," that is, established for certain groups of people, based on rite, language, nationality, or other factors (c. 518).

The canons which follow those introductory canons detail various facets of the pastoral care that is to be exercised by the pastor and those who cooperate with him, including "lay members of the Christian faithful." (See "The Meaning of 'Pastoral'" in Chapter Two: Canonical Framework.)

The Code of Canons of the Eastern Churches (1990) established a very similar set of regulations for parishes (cc. 279-303), including the pre-eminent focus on community.

In 1988 Pope John Paul II issued an apostolic exhortation *On the Vocation and the Mission of the Lay Faithful in the Church* and in the World which included a rich and varied description of parishes:

> The ecclesial community, while always having a universal dimension, finds its most immediate and visible expression in the parish. It is there that the church is seen locally. . . . it is the church living in the midst of the homes of her sons and daughters.
>
> It is necessary that in the light of the faith all discover the true meaning of the parish, that is, the place where the very "mystery" of the church is present and at work . . . The parish is not principally a structure, a territory or a building, but rather "the family of God, a fellowship afire with a unifying Spirit," "a familial and welcoming home," "the community of the faithful . . . "
>
> [I]n our day the parish still enjoys a new and promising season. As Pope Paul VI said (in 1963): "We believe simply that this old and venerable structure of the parish has an indispensable mission of great contemporary importance: to create the basic community of the Christian people; to initiate and gather the people in the accustomed expression of liturgical life; to conserve and renew the faith in the people of today; to serve as the

> school for teaching the salvific message of Christ; to put solidarity in practice and work the humble charity of good and brotherly works" (n. 26).
>
> If indeed the parish is the church placed in the neighborhoods of humanity, it lives and is at work through being deeply inserted in human society and intimately bound up with its aspirations and its dramatic events (n. 27).

When the parish, with the lay faithful's participation, adheres to its fundamental vocation and mission, it becomes a house of welcome for all and a place of service to all, or, "as Pope John XXIII was fond of saying, it is the "village fountain" to which all would have recourse in their thirst" (n. 27).

The Parish, A Collaborative Enterprise

A parish in the Catholic tradition is entrusted to a pastor for its pastoral care, but to carry out its mission in its own locale, to carry forward its many ministries, programs, and activities, the collaboration of many persons is necessary. The lay members of the parish family, in virtue of their membership in the church, are fully empowered and warmly invited to take an active part in this many-faceted project. Indeed, a central canon of the *Code of Canon Law* declares:

> The Christian faithful are those who, inasmuch as they have been incorporated in Christ through baptism, have been constituted as the people of God. For this reason, made sharers in their own way in Christ's priestly, prophetic and royal function, they are called to exercise the mission which God has entrusted to the Church to fulfill in the world, in accord with the condition proper to each (c. 204 §1).

Every member of the Church, that is to say, every parishioner who has been fully initiated by means of the sacraments of baptism, confirmation, and Holy Eucharist, and who remains in communion, possesses the Holy Spirit, and has received gifts of the Spirit. This is the source of the person's empowerment, the stimulus for the person's involvement in his or her community of faith. Being "in full communion" means to be joined with Christ in the visible structures of the Church: the profession of faith, the sacraments, and ecclesiastical governance (c. 205).

> As sharers in the mission of Christ, priest, prophet, and king, the faithful have a part to play in the life and activity of the Church . . . Nourished by their active participation in the liturgical life of their community, they are eager to share in the apostolic works of that community (*Decree on the Apostolate of the Laity*, 1965, n. 10).

The same paragraph of the Council's *Decree* goes on to say that without this active lay engagement, the pastor's apostolate, that is, his pastoral task, cannot be fully effective. Lay involvement is part and parcel of the parish community's identity, mission, and activity. This implies much more than Sunday Mass attendance and financial support. It speaks of an active participation and genuine co-responsibility.

The Church Lives by the Holy Spirit

The Second Vatican Council recovered a robust awareness of the Holy Spirit's powerful influence in the Church. The Council documents refer to the actions of the Spirit more than two hundred and fifty times. *The Dogmatic Constitution on the Church* (1964), the Council's central and controlling document, teaches this about the Spirit and the Church:

> The Spirit dwells in the church and in the hearts of the faithful as in a temple, and the Spirit prays in them and bears witness to their adoption as children of God. The Spirit leads the church into all truth and makes it one in communion and ministry, instructing and directing it through a diversity of gifts, both hierarchical and charismatic, . . . In this way the universal church appears as "a people made one by the unity of the Father and the Son and the Holy Spirit" (*Constitution on the Church*, n. 4).

Each Parishioner Is Gifted by the Spirit

It isn't only the pope and the bishops who receive the assistance of the Holy Spirit. Catholic tradition insists that every one of the baptized faithful possesses the Spirit and receives the Spirit's gifts:

> The Spirit not only sanctifies and guides the people of God by means of the sacraments and the ministries, and adorns them with virtues, the Spirit also apportions gifts "to each individually as the Spirit wills" (1 Cor 12:11), and among the faithful of every rank the Spirit distributes special graces by which they are rendered fit and ready to undertake the various offices and tasks which help the renewal and the building up of the church according to that word: "To each is given the manifestation of the Spirit for the common good" (1 Cor 12:7). These charismatic gifts, whether they be very outstanding or simpler and more widely diffused, are to be accepted with thanksgiving and consolation, since they are primarily suited to and useful for the needs of the church (*Constitution on the Church*, n. 12).

These gifts of the Spirit, along with natural abilities and acquired talents, are present in every parishioner, with wide and welcome differences. Parishioners of all ages and backgrounds have a vast range of life experiences, personal, familial, educational, professional, and employment-related. Many have serious prayer-lives, spiritual insights, and a deep commitment to their Church. The parish pastoral council strives to bring some of these gifted individuals together in an organized consultative body, so that the pastor and the parish can benefit from their wisdom and deliberations.

2: Canonical Framework for Pastoral Councils

Parish pastoral councils are firmly grounded in the law of the Church. In the section of the 1983 *Code of Canon Law* that deals with parishes, canon 536 describes the councils in these broad strokes:

1. If the diocesan bishop judges it opportune after he has heard the presbyteral council, a pastoral council is to be established in each parish, over which the pastor presides and in which the Christian faithful, together with those who share in pastoral care by virtue of their office in the parish, assist in fostering pastoral activity.

2. A pastoral council possesses a consultative vote only and is governed by the norms established by the diocesan bishop.

The Code defines the parish as a community of the Christian faithful (c. 515 §1). The parish pastoral council is an instrument of the co-responsibility of the faithful for the mission and ongoing vitality of their parish.

Unpacking the terse message of canon 536, we find the following elements: a council in every parish, made up mainly of lay parishioners, that is advisory to the pastor and works under his leadership, to promote the pastoral activity of the parish. It is required in every parish once the diocesan bishop has judged it to be opportune, and after he has sought the opinion of the presbyteral council of the diocese. As of the year 2004, 97 percent of American diocesan bishops had either mandated or encouraged parish pastoral councils (Zech [2010], 23). The bishop is to issue norms for the parish pastoral councils in the diocese which spell out the scope of their duties, the specifics of their membership, and the details of their organization and operation.

Purpose of Pastoral Councils

The purpose and task of these councils can be seen more clearly in the document of the Second Vatican Council which is their source, namely, the *Decree on the Pastoral Office of Bishops in the Church* (n. 27). The *Decree* refers explicitly to the *diocesan* pastoral council, but the Code's use of the decree as the primary source for its canon 536 on *parish* pastoral councils makes this statement of purpose in the *Decree* perfectly appropriate: "The function of this council will be to examine those matters affecting pastoral activities, to assess them and put forward practical conclusions about them."

This same passage from the *Decree* is used in canon 511 of the Code in reference to the purpose of diocesan pastoral councils; only there the English translation is slightly clearer, "In every diocese, . . . a pastoral council is to be constituted which . . . investigates, considers, and proposes practical conclusions about those things which pertain to pastoral works in the diocese."

The parish pastoral council is advisory to the pastor. It is a consultative body, not a legislative or administrative one. This is in no way a demeaning or dismissive role, "a merely advisory group." In canon law consultative bodies like parish pastoral councils are used to assist and enhance the activity of those who hold key pastoral offices at every level: the pope is advised by the synod of bishops, the bishop is advised by the diocesan pastoral council, religious superiors are similarly assisted by their councils, and so it is with parish pastors. Such consultative bodies are very important components of the canonical system. They bring to bear on pastoral matters the human insights and practical wisdom of the people, and they give voice to the gifts and graces of the Holy Spirit who dwells within each of the faithful.

Relationship to Pastor and Others

Canon 536 says that the pastor presides over the parish pastoral council. This does not imply that the pastor must chair the meetings of the council. It means that the council is subject to the pastor, it advises him, just as the president of the United States is advised by the National Security Council or the Council of Economic Advisors.

The canon also states that "those who share in pastoral care by virtue of their office in the parish" should be a part of the pastoral council. This refers specifically to parochial vicars (assistant pastors) or permanent deacons or parish life coordinators who have been assigned to the parish. It does not necessarily include the various parish staff members who are in charge of aspects of the parish's ministries like liturgy, education, or social justice. These persons, who are vitally important to the life of the parish community, should have access to the parish pastoral council when that is appropriate, but the council is not envisaged as the parish staff meeting or even as a "coordinating council" of parish ministries and activities.

The best way to characterize the parish pastoral council is that it is the principal planning group, the key group of parishioners who, with the pastor, articulate the mission of the parish, set the vision for the parish, and plan for its pastoral needs. It is not an administrative body that oversees the day-to-day operations or activities of the parish. It is a body of deeply committed, prayerful, and collaborative members of the parish who assist the pastor by planning for the future of the parish.

The importance of the parish pastoral council is highlighted by three factors:

1. It affords a permanent structure for the faithful to make known their needs, desires, and opinions to their pastors (c. 212 §§2-3).
2. It is a council, that is, a group voice whose counsel should be of greater value than that of individuals.
3. Most importantly, it has the theological value of making Christ present ("Where two or three are gathered together in my name, there I am in the midst of them," Mt 18:20), and providing more reliable access to the Holy Spirit.

The Meaning of "Pastoral"

The word "pastoral" in the title of this parish council has a very broad and general meaning. It is similar in its wide scope ("foster pastoral activity") to that of the diocesan presbyteral council ("promote the pastoral good of the people"), and to that of the diocesan pastoral council ("investigate, consider, and propose practical conclusions about those things which pertain to pastoral works").

For example, the Code assigns many pastoral responsibilities to the pastor of a parish: exercise the pastoral care of the community, carry out the functions of teaching, sanctifying, and governing (c. 519), proclaim the word of God to those in the parish and see to the Catholic education of children and youth (c. 528 §1), see that the Holy Eucharist is the center of the parish assembly and that the faithful are nourished by the celebration of the sacraments (c. 528 §2), know the faithful of the parish, visit them, share their cares and anxieties, seek out the poor, afflicted, and lonely (c. 529 §1), recognize and promote the role of the laity in the mission of the Church, and encourage the people's consciousness of belonging to the diocese and the universal Church.

The point here is the very broad meaning of the term "pastoral." Yet, its scope is not unlimited. The very existence of the parish finance council represents one such limitation. The Code requires every parish to have such a council to assist the pastor in the administration of the goods, funds, and properties of the parish (c. 537). Hence these items are not usually on the pastoral council agenda.

The Eastern Catholic Churches

The Eastern Catholic Churches, in contrast to the Latin Catholic Churches governed by the *Code of Canon Law*, have a slightly different regulation on parish councils, both pastoral and financial. Canon 295 of the *Code of Canons of the Eastern Churches*, issued in 1990 by Pope John Paul II, calls for both councils to be established in parishes in accord with the rules of each one of the autonomous Churches:

> In the parish there are to be appropriate councils dealing with pastoral and financial matters, in accord with the norms of the particular law of its own Church *sui iuris*.

The canon refers the matter of parish councils to the canonical regulations of each Eastern Church, but those rules could leave the details of the structures of the councils to the individual eparchial bishops. The point here is that these two parish councils are required in the parishes of Eastern Churches as well as those of the Latin Church, only in a slightly different way.

3: Roots in the Second Vatican Council and Subsequent Documents

Documents of the Second Vatican Council

The Second Vatican Council (1962-1965) was a "game-changing" event directed to the renewal and updating of the Roman Catholic Church. The actions taken at the Council and the documents issued by the twenty-five hundred bishops who took part in it still generate vital reflection and change in the Church. One of the central themes of the Council was that the Church is the people of God. The Christian faithful, fully incorporated into Christ by their baptism and possessing the Holy Spirit, moved to center stage, became the principal actors, with the priests and bishops serving them in their ministerial roles. Hence the emphasis on dialogue, and the emergence of organs of consultation at every level, so that active participation of the laity in all facets of the life of the Church could be made real. This theological vision was spelled out in substance and detail in the *Dogmatic Constitution on the Church* (1964), the central document of the Council.

One of the places where the Council fathers applied this theology to the practice of ministry was in the Council's *Decree on the Pastoral Office of Bishops in the Church* (1965). In this context the *Decree* stated that "in every diocese there should be established its own pastoral council . . . The function of this council will be to examine those matters affecting pastoral activities, to assess them, and to put forward practical conclusions about them" (n. 27). Note that the *Decree* referred to councils at the *diocesan* level, not at the *parish* level. Yet this is the primary source for canon 536 in the *Code of Canon Law* that calls for *parish* pastoral councils.

Implementation of the Council Decree

In August 1966, Pope Paul VI issued *Norms for the Implementation of Some Decrees of the Council* (1966). The norms were issued by way of experiment until such time as a revised *Code of Canon Law* could be formulated. The norms included this description of the purpose of *diocesan* pastoral councils.

> It is the function of the Pastoral Council to examine all matters pertaining to pastoral activities, to weigh them

carefully and to propose practical conclusions about them, so as to promote conformity to the Gospel in the life and action of the People of God (I, 16; *Canon Law Digest*, 6, 274-275).

Even though this papal directive was clearly for *diocesan* councils, the Code cited it as the second source for the canon on *parish* pastoral councils. Obviously, the drafters of the Code drew upon the pattern for diocesan pastoral councils, in both the Council *Decree* and the *Norms for Implementation*, to design councils at the parish level.

Circular Letter on Pastoral Councils

The first explicit mention of pastoral councils in *parishes* was made in a circular letter (not a legislative document) to all the bishops of the world from the Congregation for the Clergy in January 1973. The Congregation had surveyed the conferences of bishops and other Roman congregations about their views on the experiments with *diocesan* pastoral councils. The responses were positive: "the establishment of a pastoral council is important and helpful." The circular letter, approved by Pope Paul VI, provided several pages of principles and criteria for the councils, and, at the conclusion suggested that "there is nothing to prevent the institution within the diocese of councils of the same nature and function" at the parish or regional levels (*Canon Law Digest*, 8, 280-288). This tepid invitation qualified the circular letter as the third source for canon 536 of the Code.

Directory on the Office of Bishops

The fourth source document for the Code's canon on parish pastoral councils is the *Directory on the Pastoral Office of Bishops* issued in 1973 by the Congregation for Bishops. It was a pastoral handbook for bishops (also not a legislative document) offering suggestions and counsels for their ministry. It recommended the establishment of *diocesan* pastoral councils, along the lines of the preceding documents, and it explicitly linked the councils to the pastoral planning task within the diocese, but also it went one step further:

> To make the [diocesan] council's work more effective, the bishop can order, if the good of the faithful requires

it, that in every parish . . . parish councils be set up and that these be aligned with the diocesan council. These councils . . . could choose their representatives to serve on the diocesan council, so that the whole diocesan community may feel that it is offering its cooperation to its bishop through the diocesan council (*Directory*, n. 204).

Evidently, the Congregation for Bishops saw *parish* pastoral councils as lending connection and strength to *diocesan* councils, in addition to helping with the pastoral activity within the parish.

Code of Canon Law

During entire time between the conclusion of the Second Vatican Council in 1965 and the promulgation of the *Code of Canon Law* in 1983, the process for the revision of the Code was under way. The documents referred to above trace the development of the idea and outline of parish pastoral councils during that time frame. *Parish* pastoral councils were not explicitly called for by the documents of the Council, but *diocesan* pastoral councils were recommended as very desirable. Parish councils evolved *by analogy* with diocesan councils over this period of time, to such an extent that canon 536, which authorized parish pastoral councils, appeared (for the first time in the revision process) in the final draft of the Code in 1980, and emerged in exactly the same form in the actual text of the Code issued by Pope John Paul II in January 1983.

The process of development took place under the impetus of the Council's theology and spirit of renewal. The result is the parish pastoral council, a privileged instrument of consultation, an organ for lay participation and co-responsibility, and a place for pastoral planning as well as for other forms of deliberation.

Official Documents after the Code

Since the promulgation of the *Code of Canon Law* in 1983, there have been regular references to and encouragement of parish pastoral councils in official documents emanating from the popes and the congregations of the Roman Curia. They are exhortations and clarifications, not acts of legislation. It may be useful to cite them briefly.

Pope John Paul II issued an apostolic exhortation *On the Vocation and the Mission of the Lay Faithful in the Church and in the World* in 1988 after the 1987 Synod of Bishops on that topic. His exhortation explicitly and strongly encouraged parish pastoral councils as a place of collaboration between priests and people in examining and solving pastoral problems (n. 27).

In 1997 the Congregation for the Clergy and seven other offices of the Roman Curia sent out an instruction on *Certain Questions Regarding the Collaboration of the Lay Faithful in the Ministry of Priests*, in which they urged the observance of canon 536 of the Code on parish pastoral councils (art. 5, nn. 2, 3, 5).

Pope John Paul II presented an apostolic exhortation on the *Church in Asia* in 1999, following up on the Special Assembly for Asia of the Synod of Bishops held in 1998. In this document the pope spoke of parish pastoral councils as one of the participatory structures in which laity and religious should be involved in planning and decision making. "Pastoral planning with the lay faithful should be a normal feature of all parishes" (n. 25).

In 2001 Pope John Paul II issued an apostolic letter, *At the Beginning of the New Millennium*, in which he spoke of pastoral councils in the context of the notion of communion.

> The theology and spirituality of communion encourages fruitful dialogue between pastors and faithful: on the one hand uniting them *a priori* in all that is essential, and on the other leading them to pondered agreements in matters open to discussion. . . . To this end, we need to make our own the ancient pastoral wisdom, which, without prejudice to their authority, encouraged pastors to listen more widely to the entire people of God. . . . As Paulinus of Nola (d. 431) wrote, "Let us listen to what all of the faithful say because in every one of them the Spirit of God breathes."

In 2002 the Congregation for Clergy issued an instruction entitled *The Priest, Pastor and Leader of the Parish Community*, which said this about the role of the pastoral council:

> The basic task of such a [parish pastoral] council is to serve, at institutional level, the orderly collaboration

of the faithful in the development of pastoral activity which is proper to priests. The pastoral council is thus a *consultative* organin which the faithful, expressing their baptismal responsibility, can assist the parish priest, who presides at the council, by offering their advice on pastoral matters (n. 26).

It is worth noting that the updated version of the *Directory for the Pastoral Office of Bishops*, issued by the Congregation for Bishops in 2004, specifically recommends parish pastoral councils as desirable, and that every parish should have one. Through it the pastor should seek the opinions of his collaborators on questions arising in parish life (*Directory*, nn. 210-211).

4: FUNCTIONS OF THE PARISH PASTORAL COUNCIL

The function of the parish pastoral council is briefly expressed in canon 536: "The Christian faithful along with those who share in the pastoral care of the parish in virtue of their office give their help in fostering pastoral activity." Council members are to aid in the work of shepherding the flock. That puts the matter concisely. For a fuller understanding of the function of the council, we must correlate canon 536 with other official Church documents, as we have seen in the previous chapters.

Based on this correlation, we will assume that the pastoral council is a type of council, first recommended at Vatican II for *dioceses*, and that the *parish* pastoral council belongs to the same type. Vatican II's description of the function of the pastoral council in general – to investigate, to ponder, and to recommend its conclusions – applies to the parish pastoral council in particular. The council gives its help in fostering pastoral activity when the pastor consults it. He asks it to investigate and ponder some aspect of parish practice, to reach a conclusion, and to offer it to him.

In this chapter's discussion of council functions, we will look first at the council's planning function. The Church's documents state that councils have an important role to play in such planning. Next, we will examine the broad scope of the pastoral council. Pastors may consult about virtually any practical matter. Finally, we will look at the work of coordinating parish ministries, which some councils undertake.

Pastoral Planning as a Council Function

It is a commonplace that councils do pastoral planning. Planning is a shorthand expression for the threefold task of councils as defined by Vatican II. Under the pastor's direction, councils plan by investigating, reflecting, and making recommendations. A study completed in 2007 of 661 U.S. parishes found that "56 percent of the pastoral councils indicate that it is very important that they engage in planning; 43 percent agree that they are in fact very involved in pastoral planning" (Zech [2010], 51). Most councils plan. Recently, however, a question has arisen about whether "planning" correctly describes the work of the pastoral council (Hermann, 102-3). Some pastors have found planning a burdensome process. Is planning the right word to describe what councils do?

We think it is. The clearest examples of Church teaching about councils and planning come from the Congregation for Bishops. In its 1973 *Directory on the Pastoral Ministry of Bishops* (n. 204), the congregation had this to say about the diocesan pastoral council:

> By its study and reflection, the council furnishes the judgments necessary to enable the diocesan community to plan its pastoral program systematically and to fulfill it effectively.

The Congregation for Bishops was envisioning that diocesan pastoral councils could help bishops plan. The congregation reaffirmed this point in its 2004 *Directory for Bishops* (n. 184). In the newer *Directory*, the Congregation had this to say about diocesan pastoral councils and planning:

> The Bishop may propose themes for the council to discuss in connection with the pastoral activity of the diocese: these include the pastoral plan, various catechetical, missionary and apostolic initiatives, ways of improving the doctrinal formation and sacramental life of the faithful, assistance for the pastoral ministry of the clergy, and various means of raising public awareness regarding concerns of the Church.

In this passage, we see a direct connection between the diocesan pastoral council and the pastoral plan. The bishop may request a thorough discussion of it. So we can say that official documents link diocesan pastoral councils and planning.

Our assumption is that the pastoral council is a single type of council recommended for parishes as well as dioceses. The parish pastoral council functions in the same way as the diocesan pastoral council, doing so at the parochial level. If planning is the work of the diocesan pastoral council, it is no less the work of the parish pastoral council.

To be sure, official church documents do not directly equate the work of pastoral councils with pastoral planning. The function of the council depends on how the pastor consults it. Official documents state, however, that councils have an important role to play in such planning. Investigating and reflecting on a topic, and recommending the conclusions to the pastor, a council has a task broader than pastoral planning, but the council's task should include it.

If pastoral planning is a function of pastoral councils, how do we define it? One author has summarized the pastoral planning task in this way:

> A pastoral council reads the signs of the times and devises the actions of the faith community, the Body of Christ, to respond to the discerned pastoral issues and needs. The essential work of a pastoral council is to participate with the pastor or pastoral leader in thinking and praying about these actions (Pickett, 31).

According to this author, thinking and praying about these actions "is" pastoral planning. Popular authors and official Church documents agree that planning as a function of pastoral councils.

Scope of the Pastoral Council

Another way to speak of the function of the parish pastoral council is to describe its scope. Local Church guidelines for parish pastoral councils, as well as popular books and articles, indicate the breadth of the council. Indeed, there are almost no limits to the scope of the pastoral council. The pastor may invite the council to study virtually any practical matter. But there is one significant limit. Councils do not examine theoretical questions. It is "beyond the competence" of councils, said the Congregation for the Clergy (1973, n. 9), "to decide on general questions bearing on faith, orthodoxy, moral principles or laws of the universal Church." Councils are to concentrate on practical matters. The field of practical activities is quite broad, and within it councils enjoy a wide scope.

Lists of potential pastoral council activities, however, can mislead readers into thinking that the council functions independently of the pastor. This would be a serious mistake. Just because one council evaluates parish programs, or develops a parish policy, or facilitates communication, does not mean that every council can or should do so. The subject matter of the council depends on the pastor. He is the one who consults. The council responds to his request, and is not a law unto itself. To be sure, council members should speak frankly, and should freely propose topics for consideration by the council. But the pastoral council was never intended to be an open forum or a sounding board. The right of all parishioners to speak to their pastors is guaranteed apart from the pastoral council. Such councils were not created as a remedy for breakdowns in communication, but to assist the pastor's apostolate of shepherding the community.

The relationship between pastor and council is important to consider when we read examples from official documents about how pastoral councils can give their help. Councils may present to the pastor proposals and suggestions about the church's mission, catechesis, sacramental life, and even matters of public opinion (Cong. Clergy [1973], n. 9). But these are examples. The Church does not envision that every pastoral council will undertake these tasks. Council members may propose such themes to a pastor for possible consideration by the council. They become actual matter for the council when the pastor accepts the council's proposal. Pastors have the prerogative of consulting the council as they see fit. The Church does not obligate pastors to accept the pastoral council's advice.

This brings us back to the consultative relationship between pastors and councils. A pastor consults the pastoral council, we said, because he has a question. The question may be a broad one, such as "What are the spiritual needs of this parish?" Thinking even more broadly, the pastor might ask the council itself to propose topics for consideration. Broad questions are at one end of the spectrum. At the other end are more narrow questions. A pastor may ask, "What is the most effective way to upgrade the parish's heating and cooling system?" This question is very narrow. But whether broad or narrow, the question always remains the pastor's.

The matter for discussion is a "pastoral" matter because it pertains to his apostolate as the chief shepherd. The pastor invites the council to address the question in the threefold way defined at Vatican II. The council investigates, ponders, and recommends conclusions. Accepting his invitation, the council members put their gifts at the service of the parish. The council succeeds, we can say, when its recommendations are so prudent that the pastor gladly accepts and implements them. Success means that the council has fostered pastoral activity in the threefold way specific to the council.

Do Pastoral Councils "Coordinate" and "Implement"?

A survey of 661 U.S. Catholic parishes in 2007 noted that many pastoral councils understand their job as coordinating parish activities:

> Forty-two percent of the parish pastoral councils in our sample believe that it is very important the council coordinate parish activities; 31 percent indicate that the council is very involved in coordinating parish activities (Zech [2010], 51).

The number of parishes whose councils coordinate is smaller than those whose councils plan, but it is significant. The "coordinating" council is sometimes called "the council of ministries" (Sweetser, 126). It understands itself as a body of representatives from a variety of the parish's ministerial groups. The council makes policy for the groups and coordinates them through a system of standing committees.

In some parishes, pastoral councils try to both plan and coordinate (Zech [2010], 26). Moreover, some councils also implement the activities that they recommend. This can create problems. Asking the pastoral council to both implement and coordinate parish activities, as well as to do pastoral planning, is a tall order. The authors of the 2007 survey wrote that implementing and coordinating "is a lot to ask of a group of volunteers who typically only meet once a month" (Zech [2010], 26). Some pastors might object, however, that they lack the human resources to implement what councils recommend. For that reason, they ask the council members to carry out the council's proposals. But planning itself is no small task. If the council does not itself intend to implement what it recommends, it should consider who will implement the recommendations. It should assess the resources to implement the plan.

There is a further problem. To say that the pastoral council should oversee and implement parish activities appears to contradict its nature as a consultative body. Instead it seems to assign to pastoral councils an executive or supervisory function. Here canon law is very specific: councils have a "consultative vote only," and lack the authority to implement things independently. How are we to understand the council as consultative when the council both oversees and implements?

To answer this question we have recourse to the broad terms of canon 536. The pastoral council is to "give its help in fostering pastoral activity." Oversight and implementation may fall under this rubric. Pastors who consult councils may ask them to give their help in the parish apostolate by overseeing and implementing. When they offer this help, however, they do so as consultants, and not as parish staff members.

We conclude that the authentic vision from the Council is that of a planning group. If and whenever possible, that should be the pastoral council's priority agenda. But since the pastoral council is also a consultative body and an organ of participation of the laity in the pastoral activity of the parish, other matters may be brought to it for measured advice. Its agenda is not rigidly limited to planning. Coordination of parish organizations, programs, and activities, is another sort of administrative/managerial function, although one not well suited to an investigative, reflective, practical consultative group.

Summary: The Pastor and the Council's Functions

Pastors may consult their councils in a variety of ways, asking them to assume a great many practical functions. Of these, the best-attested council function is the threefold task as described in the Vatican II *Decree on the Pastoral Office Bishops in the Church* (n. 27) and reinforced by subsequent official documents. At the pastor's request, pastoral councils investigate and reflect on some matter and offer their conclusions in the form of recommendations. This threefold task can be equated with pastoral planning, a term also affirmed by official documents.

Pastoral council functions have their context in the relationship between the pastor and the council. He consults the members, and they put their gifts at the service of the parish. Consultation is a broad term. It may even include the oversight and implementation of parish activities, even though these seem to be executive functions. Essential to the pastoral council, however, is that it does not exercise its functions independent of the pastor. Consulting the council, the pastor asks it to help foster pastoral activity. This help is not an autonomous pastoral council function. It is a response to the pastor's request. He consults the members, asking them how best to strengthen the pastoral apostolate. The council succeeds when its recommendations are so wise and good that the pastor accepts them and acts upon them. In the next chapter, we will examine the relationship between the pastor and the council, and between the council and other groups in the parish.

5: PARISH PASTORAL COUNCIL RELATIONSHIPS

The words of canon 536 express a relationship between the pastor and the council. The canon states that he "presides" over the council, and adds that it possesses only a "consultative vote." In other words, it exercises initiative, but does so when the pastor consults it. The council has a vote, but it does not have deliberative authority. It does not legislate for the parish. The pastor turns to the council as to a consultant. He asks for something from the council, i.e., help in fostering pastoral activity. The council is not independent of him.

The relationship between the pastor and the council is the most important of all council relationships. Although council members interact with other parishioners, and may have special dealings with the finance council and the staff, the relationship to the pastor is primary. In this chapter, we will first lay out the relationship between the pastor and the council. Then we will look at the secondary relationships between the council and other individuals and groups in the parish.

The Primary Relationship

The pastor consults the pastoral council. Council members give their help by responding to his requests. The two have a reciprocal relationship. The council exists, we could say, precisely so that the pastor might consult it.

This basic insight has important consequences for understanding the pastoral nature of the council. The pastor, as the one who consults the council, approaches it with implicit expectations. He consults because he wants something from it that he cannot otherwise obtain. What he seeks from the council could not be expert advice. The council is not mainly a body of experts, chosen for their technical knowledge. To be sure, the council may include experts, and the pastor can undoubtedly benefit from them. But he must be expecting from the council something other than technical expertise, something like prudence or practical wisdom. He asks for recommendations about how he should act in a given situation of the parish. Council members have knowledge of the parish and sensitivity to its needs. That is what the pastor seeks.

Consulting the council, the pastor expects it to do something specific. He expects it to accomplish its threefold mission. He invites the members to investigate some aspect of the parish reality and reflect on it, so that the council can reach a decision about the matter. Then it can offer the pastor its conclusions in the form of recommendations. In the act of consulting, the pastor directs the council members' attention. He defines the matter about which he wants to consult. He should explain why it is important and why it has consequences for the parish and its mission. When the council members understand the pastor's question, investigate it and reflect on what they have learned, they can formulate a conclusion that will help him.

Also implicit in the relationship between the pastor and the council is trust. By consulting, the pastor puts his trust in the council. He expresses his confidence that the council will do what it is meant to do. The growth of trust takes time. Pastors have to learn the capabilities of the council. They have to discover the talents of the individual members, and assess their ability to work together. This will affect the matter about which the pastor consults, for the wise pastor does not ask the council to undertake something beyond its capabilities. It also has consequences for the selection of council members, as we will see in a later chapter. Effective councils are composed of members who are capable of doing the council's threefold work: investigating, reflecting, and making recommendations.

In short, the consultative nature of the pastoral council suggests that the pastor approaches it with a question. He expects the council to investigate, reflect, and draw conclusions. If the council's advice is prudent, he will accept its advice, and his trust in the council will grow.

The consultative nature of the council also implies something about the council's motive. The members share in the apostolate or role of the pastor. They do so by responding to his request to examine some aspect of parish life and make recommendations. Councils succeed when their advice to the pastor is so wise and good that he accepts and implements it. It is important for the council to understand what the pastor is asking. If the members do not understand, they will not know how they are to investigate and apply the knowledge they gain. Moreover, the conclusions they draw may be irrelevant to the pastor's question. Council members understand that they are consultants. The pastor consults them because he wants their help. The value of their work depends on the contribution it makes to the mission of the parish.

The documents of the Church imply that the council has a specific role to play. Council meetings should not be mere open forums or unstructured discussions. They are rather opportunities for the pastor to pose his questions and for the council to respond in a definite way. When a pastor asks the council to investigate a matter, he should help the council to see what a good investigation entails, and what the council needs in order to carry it out. This implies "study and consideration" (Cong. Clergy [1973], n. 4) as well as "suitable preparation" (Cong. Bishops [2004], n. 184). The council's reflections are meant to lead to a conclusion. Official documents of the Church do not specify how to reach this conclusion, and do not express a preference for parliamentary procedure or other ways to seek consensus. But it is clear that council members are meant to recommend to the pastor their conclusions. That implies a specific ability on the part of members. They must be able to compromise with one another and reach agreement.

In summary, the relationship between the council and the pastor is primary. He consults because he seeks the council's practical wisdom on a given issue. The members respond in the specific threefold manner of the pastoral council. Trust should exist between the pastor and the council. When the pastor accepts its recommendations and implements them, the council has successfully achieved its mission.

Secondary Relationships

Parishioners. The pastoral council has other relationships, apart from its relationship with the pastor. It has a relationship, for example, with the entire parish. The council can be said to "represent" the parish in a special way. It represents the wisdom of the community and offers it to the pastor. Speaking of diocesan pastoral councils, a 1973 Vatican document described its "representative" character in this way:

> Although the members of the council cannot in a juridical sense be called representatives of the total diocesan community, nevertheless, as far as possible, they should present a witness or sign of the entire diocese (Cong. Clergy, [1973] n. 7).

What was said about *diocesan* pastoral councils can also be said about *parish* pastoral councils: the council is a sign of the wisdom of the entire parish. That does not mean, however, that its members represent the parish as elected legislators represent their constituencies. They are not like city council members who represent a precinct or district. Even less does it imply that the pastoral council should report to parishioners about its deliberations. Council members are consultants of the pastor. He may report to the parish about the results of his consultation, but council members are not meant to do so on their own. The council is not an independent representative body.

Because the pastoral council has a representative function (in that it strives to "make present" the wisdom of the community), it will necessarily relate to parish committees, organizations, and ministries led by volunteers. The council relates to them by knowing them. Council members should be aware of the leaders and principal initiatives of parish life. Pastors consult councils about what to do in a parish whose very life resides in the actions and aspirations of its people. When parishioners tell council members about their life and ministry, the members should listen closely.

Parish Staff. Canon 536 states that parish officials "give their help in fostering pastoral activity." These officials are the clergy – priests and deacons – who hold an assigned office. The council may also include parish staff. This implies the presence on the council of religious and laity employed by the parish, such as sisters who work in the parish and members of the parish staff. It is not necessary that every parish staff member belong to the pastoral council. After all, the pastor may consult his staff at any time, and need not incorporate its members in the pastoral council. The pastor may do so, however, as the need arises. He may also invite parish staff members to attend council meetings when the council discusses matter of which the staff member has expertise.

Earlier we said that the pastor, in consulting the council, seeks prudence or practical wisdom, as distinct from technical expertise. Practical wisdom is knowledge about how to act rightly in a specific situation, in comparison to the kinds of knowledge that one can gain from consulting a textbook, knowledge that claims to be always and everywhere true. This distinction is important in understanding the relationship between the council and the parish staff or other expert groups, such as the parish finance council. Pastors who seek advice about a technical matter – parish maintenance, finances, liturgical music, catechetics, for example – might be better off consulting the staff rather than the pastoral council. The parish staff and the finance council may have specialized knowledge about the pastor's matter of concern. When a matter falls within their areas of expertise, he would do well to ask their advice.

Finance Council. The prudence or practical wisdom of the pastoral council is not tied to a specific discipline. It is rather a general capability – the ability to know the parish and its people, and to discern the best choice of action in a given situation. This distinguishes the pastoral council from the finance council. Members of the finance council should have expertise in the administration of ecclesiastical goods, e.g., in law, accounting, and finance. The threefold duty of the pastoral council is more general.

How are we to describe the relationship between the pastoral and finance councils? Is one council superior to the other? These questions have been widely discussed. Some authors have argued for a strict division between the two councils, with "administrative matters" off-limits for the pastoral council (Keating, 264; Kim, 48; and Griese, 53). Other authors recommend that that the finance council should be a committee of the pastoral council (Sweetser, 164-165; Rademacher [1979], 103). These arguments tend to overlook the consultative nature of both councils. One is not superior to the other. Rather, the pastor consults the finance council about the administration of parish goods. He consults the pastoral council about practical matters that require investigation and reflection. If the two councils give the pastor conflicting advice, he must make a decision. The decision cannot be made in advance on account of the hypothetical superiority of one council over another.

To sum up, the pastoral council includes the parish clergy, such as parochial vicars and deacons. It may also include religious employed by the parish, and other staff members. But their membership is not required. The general principle is that the pastor will consult as he sees fit. Staff members have special expertise, and the pastor may need their advice about matters that require such expertise. The finance council is another source of expert knowledge. The pastor will consult it about questions of administration, law, accounting, and financial reporting. The pastoral council, by comparison, has a more general field of responsibility. The pastor consults it, not primarily to gain expert opinion, but to discover practical wisdom. The pastoral council advises about how best to act in a situation that is governed by the changing needs of the community.

Summary: Primary and Secondary Relationships

The pastoral council's threefold mission of investigating, reflecting, and recommending will certainly bring it into contact with the parishioners at large, as well as with the parish staff and the finance council. All of these, however, are secondary relationships. The pastoral council relates primarily to the pastor. He defines the matter for consultation, and the council responds by offering its gifts of study and discernment. Although the council is said to represent the parish, it does not do so as a legislature or independent commission. It represents the parish by making present the wisdom of the People of God. This points to the importance of selecting council members, which is the topic of the next chapter.

6: MEMBERSHIP IN THE PARISH PASTORAL COUNCIL

Canon 536 says that the parish pastoral council is to be composed of "the Christian faithful along with those who share in the pastoral care of the parish by virtue of their offices in the parish." The canon does not say how to select the members. Canon 512, about *diocesan* pastoral councils, sheds light on the question of *parish* pastoral council membership. It states, "The pastoral council consists of Christian faithful who are in full communion with the Catholic Church." This assertion about diocesan councils applies to the parish also. Parish pastoral council members should be fully participating members of the Catholic community.

This chapter will consider the membership of the parish pastoral council. We will look first at its representative nature. Then we will consider the various ways proposed for selecting members. Finally, we will see what motivates parishioners to serve on the council.

Representation

Canon 512 suggests the representative nature of the diocesan pastoral council. It says that the membership should include "clerics, members of institutes of consecrated life and especially lay persons." This is especially important at the diocesan level, where the number of council members, drawn from the entire diocese, may be larger. Representation at the parish level, however, is also relevant. Canon 512 states:

> The Christian faithful who are appointed to the pastoral council are to be so selected that the entire portion of the people of God which constitutes the diocese is truly reflected, with due regard for the diverse regions, social conditions and professions of the diocese as well as the role which they have in the apostolate, either as individuals or in conjunction with others.

This passage about the diocesan pastoral council suggests that the parish pastoral council should also be representative to some extent. In 1983, when the *Code* was published, representation meant diversity: geographic diversity, economic and occupational diversity, and diversity in the apostolate or ministry. Today we would add racial, ethnic, and gender diversity.

Church documents do not consider the pastoral council a representative body in the juridical sense, as we saw in the previous chapter. Councils are not representative assemblies. Canon 512 states that *diocesan* councils are to reflect "the entire portion of the people of God." That may be the goal of the *parish* council as well. It "represents" the parish community in that its members make present the wisdom of God residing within it.

Occasionally council members will complain that their fellow parishioners hardly know of the council. This complaint may reflect the conviction that the pastoral council, if it is to be truly representative, should be a clearly visible and public body. According to this conviction, it represents the parish, just as a city council represents the civil electorate. But let us recall from Chapter Five that the pastoral council's relationship to other parishioners is subordinate to its relationship to the pastor. He consults the council as part of his own apostolate or role, distinct from the apostolate of the laity. Primarily, the council is to relate to him, and only secondarily to the rest of the parish.

Selection of Members

Neither canon 536 or 512 explains how to choose pastoral council members. Canon 536 simply says that, if a bishop "judges it opportune" (after listening to the presbyteral council), "a pastoral council is to be established in each parish." Canon 512 (about diocesan councils) states that council members are to be "selected" and "appointed." The verbs simply suggest that candidates who are "chosen" are first "considered" for membership.

Election. In recent years, opinion seems to have shifted regarding the election of council members at large. After councils were first established in the USA, and for decades thereafter, the most common way of selecting members was via at-large parish elections. Although such general elections remain the most common way to select members, many dioceses now recommend the election "or" the appointment of members. A growing number of parishes utilize a more complicated process that involves a communal "discernment" of pastoral council members (Zech [2010], 55-59).

Discernment. The value of discernment becomes obvious when we consider the skills that a pastoral council member needs to accomplish the council's threefold role. The competent council member should have the curiosity and tenacity to investigate a matter thoroughly. Such a councillor must also have the patience and thoughtfulness to reflect upon the investigation's relevance to the parish. And finally, competent council members will be able to reach a group decision, which implies the ability to compromise and seek consensus. By contrast, popular and outgoing parishioners – the kind often chosen in an at-large election – may not have these skills. A process of discernment may yield more promising nominees than a general election.

Typically, communal discernment of council members involves the establishment of a nominations committee. The committee identifies promising candidates, either by itself or at an open parish meeting. It interviews them and weighs their potential contribution to the council (McKinney, 100-103). The actual selection of council members might be done by the nominations committee itself, or by the participants at an open parish meeting, or by the pastor, who appoints the members. The process of discernment is less common than an at-large election, but seems to be growing in popularity.

Choice by Parish Organizations. Another common way to select pastoral council members is to allow standing committees in the parish, or parish organizations, to make the choice. This is the defining feature of the council known as the "council of ministries," as we saw in the previous chapter. In this style of council, the members represent the various parish ministries, and the council coordinates them and makes policy for them. The council of ministries tends to exercise an executive function that does not easily harmonize with the consultative nature of the pastoral council. But the selection of council members through standing committees or parish organizations is popular.

Appointment by the Pastor. The appointment of councillors by the pastor is also very common. In almost one-half of all councils, the pastor appoints at least one member. Guidelines commonly explain this practice as a way of maintaining "balance" in the pastoral council. It allows pastors to hand-pick members who should belong to the council in order to achieve "balance among sexes, ethnic groups, age groups, and areas of knowledge and competence desired of the Council" (Zech [2010], 58). Pastors want to consult the people whose wisdom they value. By appointing members, they can ensure the participation of those who might be overlooked in an at-large election.

Ex Officio Members. Finally, some pastoral council members are chosen on account of their office. *Ex officio* council members were reported in almost 50 percent of 661 parishes surveyed in 2010. Mistakenly, some parishes listed the pastor as an *ex officio* member of the council – as if he were not the legal representative of the parish and the one who is consulting. But the pastor is not a member of the pastoral council. He does not vote, not even to break ties. Instead he receives the recommendations of the council. Its *ex officio* members include parochial vicars, permanent deacons, and frequently religious sisters assigned to the parish as well as other staff members. Canon law does not require all of them to be members of the pastoral council, but some of them frequently are.

In short, the most common method for selecting councillors is to elect them at large. A growing number of diocesan guidelines for councils recommend the selection of members through a process of discernment. This can mean that they are nominated by a committee or at a general parish meeting. The actual selection may be made by the committee or by the pastor, or new members may be discussed and chosen at an open parish meeting. A quarter of parishes report that their members are selected to represent parish committees or organizations. Pastors appoint some members in almost half of all parishes. And finally, many councils include members who are present *ex officio*.

The Motivation of Parishioners

Pastors occasionally complain that councils do not do enough work, or that parishioners do not want to fill vacancies in the council. These complaints deserve attention. Let us first consider the situation in which councils do not perform adequate work. Recall that council members have the duty of investigating carefully, reflecting thoroughly, and recommending their conclusions. Pastors who are dissatisfied with the council should identify the point of dissatisfaction. Perhaps the council does not understand what it is to investigate, or how it is to do so. The pastor has a right and an obligation to explain to members their duties. The members' success hinges upon the quality of their advice. If their recommendations are sound, and the pastor acts on them, that will motivate parishioners to join the council. If the recommendations are unsound, he should explain why he cannot accept them and ask for further investigation and reflection. Many times the pastor who complains about the council's work has failed to explain what he wants from the council.

The second source of frustration for pastors is the unwillingness of parishioners to serve on the council. Parishioners often plead that prior obligations prevent them from serving. The pastor can motivate them, however, by announcing in advance what he wishes to consult about. The announcement may attract parishioners with an interest in the topic of consultation. They may want to share their insights about a matter of consequence to the parish. Parishioners rarely want to join a council whose meetings consist of general discussions or open forums. But they indeed may want to participate in a council that seeks recommendations which the pastor can accept and implement. If pastors announce new initiatives to the parish at large by saying that they were recommended by the pastoral council, the announcement may motivate parishioners to join when vacancies occur.

Number, Term, and Replacement

Number. Neither canon law nor the documents of the Church specify the number of members that a pastoral council should have. In this case, practice should guide theory. A survey of 661 U.S. Catholic parishes reports that the typical pastoral council has approximately 12 members. In larger parishes, parishes in the Northeast, and urban parishes, the pastoral councils tend to have 13 to 15 council members (Zech [2010], 55). Pastors who invite their councils to investigate, reflect, and draw conclusions need enough members to do the work, but not so many that it is difficult to reach agreements (Cong. Clergy [1973], n. 7).

Term. Official documents do not specify a term of office for pastoral council members. The 1973 Circular Letter of the Congregation for Clergy suggests, however, that the term should be limited. This gives veteran council members a graceful opportunity to bring their service to an end, and offers new people an opportunity to serve on the council. It is common for people to serve a two- or three-year term. In addition, the Congregation for the Clergy has recommended that pastoral council members (apart from clergy) should be "nominated for a period of time determined in the statutes." (Cong. Clergy [1973], n. 7).

Replacement. The word "statutes" refers to norms or pastoral council guidelines established by the diocesan bishop (c. 94). If diocesan norms or guidelines do not define a term of office for pastoral council members, an individual council could define the term in a constitution or bylaw. They can also define how to remove or replace members who are unable or unwilling to perform their duties (by missing meetings without good reason, physical or mental incapacity, or failure to perform council duties). The Congregation for the Clergy has also recommended a staggered system of terms, with some new members periodically coming on and going off. Pastors benefit by attracting new council members (Cong. Clergy [1973], n. 7).

In summary, the Code does not explain how to choose parish pastoral members. It wants pastoral councils in general to be "representative," but only says that the membership should be geographically, economically, occupationally, and apostolically diverse. Church documents do not speak of "demographic" diversity. They do not consider councils to be representative bodies in the juridical sense. Instead, they represent the faithful by making present the wisdom of God alive in the parish community.

The general principle that governs the selection of the pastoral council is this: pastors consult because they want the council's help in studying and considering a matter. They should consult those whose advice they value. The best and most successful council is the one whose advice is so wise and prudent that the pastor willingly accepts it. Every method of choosing pastoral council members should aim at attracting councillors who can offer that advice. They are the ones who know the parish and are capable of accomplishing the council's threefold role.

7: Operation of the Parish Pastoral Council

In Chapter Four, we looked at the functions of the parish pastoral council. We saw that pastoral council members "give their help in fostering pastoral activity" (c. 536). We then expanded this insight by examining the diocesan pastoral council. It has the duty "to investigate under the authority of the bishop all those things which pertain to pastoral works, to ponder them and to propose practical conclusions about them" (c. 511). Canon 511 (about diocesan councils) amplifies canon 536 (about parish councils).The parish council offers its help in fostering pastoral activity by investigating, under the pastor's authority, things that pertain to the ministry of parish leadership (i.e., "pastoral work"). It reflects on them and proposes its conclusions. Council members, in short, are pastoral planners. That is their *function*.

This chapter will focus on the *operation* of the council, that is, the way it carries out its function. To begin, we must recall that the pastor consults the council. Serving the pastoral ministry is the council's reason for being. The pastor seeks from council members their prudence, common sense, and practical wisdom. The pastor's search is the foundation for council operations. The council operates – it accomplishes its work – by starting with the pastor. What decisions does he face? What would he like the council to investigate? How would the council apply what it has learned to the matter that the parish faces? When the council answers these questions, its work can begin.

Collaborating with the Pastor

The importance of the pastor to council operations cannot be overemphasized. Since he consults, and since council members recommend their conclusions to him, the success of the consultation depends on his approval. He has to judge the council's investigation sufficient and its discernment sound. He alone can accept its advice. When the pastor does so, the council has accomplished its work. For that reason, the pastor should be a part of the council's operations at every stage, approving its general direction and affirming its methods. The pastor should even prescribe for the council the form in which he would like to receive its conclusions, whether expressed as a written report, as the development of a policy, or as oral answers to his questions. The pastoral council never operates in a manner wholly independent of the pastor. It collaborates with him. The success of its operation depends on the acceptance that he alone can give.

In the past, some writers have proposed that pastoral councils should take a comprehensive approach to the parish's activity and ministerial well-being. One proposal states that the essence of parish life consists of seven elements: evangelization, worship, word, community, service, stewardship, and leadership. The agenda of the council is "to research, consider and propose for action those matters considered to be truly 'pastoral,' those matters that directly relate to the seven elements" (Gubish, 63). Pastoral councils then assess the parish's strengths in each of the seven areas. A second proposal states that parishes should establish a committee for each ministerial area. In this council of ministries, there should be a committee for spiritual life and worship, Christian formation, social ministry, administrative services, and parish and community life. The proposal calls these standing committees of the pastoral council. The council coordinates them, directing them and holding them accountable (Rademacher [1988], 98). These two proposals give the pastoral council a specific operation, either comprehensive planning (in the one case) or committee supervision (in the other).

Such proposals can suggest that the pastoral council has a role independent of the pastor. They imply that the pastoral council has the duty of comprehensive planning, or the duty of coordinating ministerial committees – duties that are obligatory for the council, whether or not the pastor has requested the council to perform them. But the pursuit of a council agenda distinct from the concerns of the pastor can be counterproductive. At least one pastoral team has complained that the planning agenda of its council "focuses primarily on the parish, its programs and its activities" and neglects "to ponder the massive changes occurring in the lives of the people" (Hermann, 103). According to this complaint, the council had its own agenda, pastoral planning, which was not what the pastor had asked. He wanted to consult the council about something else. So when we speak of the operation of the pastoral council, we do not mean that it has responsibilities apart from the work that the pastor has asked it to do. No council should assume that its work is laid out in a guidebook or manual, quite apart from the pastor.

Prudence and Practical Wisdom

Let us assume that the pastor has shared with the council members a particular concern. He has a decision to make about some parish matter, and wants to make the correct one. It does not hinge upon a technical issue about which he could consult an expert or a staff member. It does not hinge upon the correct application of principles that he could learn from a textbook. No, it has to do with something intangible: with the spirit of the community, with its faith and morale, and with its potential for growth and change. About these matters, no expert has the final word. For these things, the pastor wants to consult with people who know the parish well.

In matters that require prudence, a correct decision depends on the needs of the parish. These needs may vary from year to year. To be sure, some things remain constant. The pastor always needs to preach the Word, to celebrate the sacraments, and to pay the bills. But apart from these constants, parish needs vary. The pastor may ask whether he should invest in a new program or raise money for a building. He may have received complaints about a ministry or an aspect of parish life, and wonder how to respond to them. He may have a hope to re-evangelize his community, renew the liturgy, or strengthen youth ministry – and seeks counsel about how to do these things effectively. To be sure, experts can instruct him. And pastors do well to consult their fellow clergy and the experts on the parish staff. But pastoral councils do not operate by offering the expert advice that professionals can give. They operate by sharing their own practical wisdom. Sometimes the right decision depends on weighing carefully the decision's pros and cons. The pastor needs collaborators with whom he can dialogue. In the dialogue, they bring matters to light that he may never have considered. Sharing this kind of wisdom may help the pastor to understand the community and its needs, and ultimately to make a prudent decision.

So when we speak of the operation of the council, we do not mean that it must follow an inflexible method. Its method is rather the freedom of dialogue. The conversation partners follow the subject matter, wherever it leads them. The pastor and the council should be free to pursue the truth of the matter. This can sometimes be difficult. The council's investigation may reveal things that are painful to acknowledge, and its reflection may suggest needed changes if the parish is to be faithful to the Gospel. But this is why ecclesial consultation is desirable. Love and care for the parish unite pastors and their council members, impelling them to clearly see the reality of the parish. When the spirit of truth leads, an honest dialogue results.

Conduct of Meetings

The conduct of council meetings usually follows a set of by-laws or a foundational document created by the council. To ensure the success of meetings, the pastor and leaders should plan them thoroughly. This preparation typically involves the preparation of a prayer, reflection or Scripture reading for the beginning and end of meetings. It also involves the establishment in advance of a written agenda, the facilitation of the meeting by a skilled chairperson, and an honest account of the meeting by a secretary.

Agenda. A well-developed agenda is more than a list of topics for discussion. It also indicates how the discussion is to proceed, and enables council members to prepare for the discussion in advance. Council meetings can involve a variety of activities. For example, the council can impart information and give reports. In this activity, one person speaks and the others listen. Members can also dialogue with one another, brainstorming and exchanging opinions. At a more challenging level, members can argue for a point of view, offering reasons for their convictions. At the most difficult level, the council members can attempt to reach a decision, by voting or by seeking consensus. Each of these types of activities requires different skills. The agenda, by indicating not only the topic but the process by which the discussion will proceed, enables members to prepare for the meeting.

Facilitation. The pastor presides at the pastoral council meetings. Ultimately he receives the recommendations of the members. But he may not want to facilitate the meeting or serve as the chairman. It is common for a member of the council to assume that responsibility. The chairperson or facilitator typically meets with the pastor and other council officers to plan the agenda, and then conducts the meeting, freeing the pastor to listen or speak as he sees fit. Chairpersons are responsible for the meeting's good order. They closely follow the agenda, ensuring that everyone has a chance to speak and be heard. The chair may conduct the meeting by parliamentary procedure (Howes, 50), or the council may decide matters by a process of spiritual discernment (McKinney, 41-47). When an agenda item appears to require more time than what is available, the chairperson may propose a halt to the discussion and its postponement it to a later meeting.

Record-Keeping. Maintaining a good record of the pastoral council meeting allows the group to monitor its own progress and prepare for the future. Record-keeping is the duty of the secretary. The secretary, by keeping track of council conversations, enables the council to reflect precisely on its past business. This is especially helpful when the time comes to plan its next meeting. By consulting the minutes, planners can judge how much the council achieved at its last meeting, and how much it was unable to accomplish. For example, the council may have been able to weigh the pros and cons of a matter, without deciding the issue. The agenda for the next meeting might explain that the council will take a vote on the matter or engage in a process for further discernment.

The Pastor and Planning

When a pastor introduces a matter to the pastoral council, he should aim to help the council see the matter clearly. The council needs to understand why it is an issue for him and the parish. The pastor should explain why he wants to consult the council, and why he hopes that it can shed light on the matter before him. Then he can ask the council to begin its work of study, reflection, and attaining consensus.

The first task of the council is investigation. The pastor must show the members what kind of investigation would be most helpful. He may have to identify for the council members how he would like them to investigate. Perhaps he wants them to read about the matter in a book or in an article. Perhaps he wants them to consult with experts, with neighboring parishes, or with diocesan officials. Perhaps he wants them to consult the parishioners through a questionnaire, or an open meeting, or even by means of guided conversations or "appreciative inquiry" (DeLambo, 87-101). Whatever approach the council takes, its first task is to investigate, that is, to discover the truth. That is why the Church's official documents speak of the council's need for study and consideration as well as for "suitable preparation" (Cong. Bishops [2004], n. 184). Since the pastor hopes to benefit from the process, he should decide how much investigation is enough. In this process, the council should be able to do its work thoroughly.

Then, after the council has educated itself about the matter, it has to reflect. The pastor is not interested in the amassing of facts by themselves.

He is looking for a practical recommendation. So as the council reports to him what it has learned, he must consider its relevance. How does the council's investigation shed light on the issue faced by the parish or on the decision that the pastor must make? How does it decide whether the parish has the resources necessary to accomplish a new initiative? In this case, the literature about group process is relevant (McKinney, 41-47; Pickett, 226-233; Olsen, 81-97). There are many ways in which council members can digest, analyze, absorb, and synthesize what they have learned. Their conversation can reveal the differing consequences of making one decision or another. Council members will see things that the pastor may not see, and help him to understand them.

Finally, the council has to reach a conclusion and recommend it to the pastor. This is the most difficult step. Councillors face the challenge of reaching a single mind about a matter, or at least of attaining a compromise that the entire council can affirm. This is no easy achievement, for members are not simply trying to please themselves, but recommending a course of action that the pastor can accept. They strive to be, not just of one mind among themselves, but also of one mind with the pastor. Since he is consulting them, he should explain what kind of advice he seeks and provide the necessary information. That will help the council to understand the issues he faces, and to offer the kind of advice and support that he needs.

The Council's Operation

The parish pastoral council carries out its threefold function of investigating, reflecting, and recommending. The pastor consults it and seeks its prudent advice. He and the council seek the truth of a matter. A thorough dialogue may help him to act wisely on behalf of the parish (Paul VI [1964], section III).

On occasion, council members may disagree with the pastor. When their advice is unanimous it is wise for the pastor to explain why he does not accept it. On those occasions he should give the reasons why he cannot accept a council recommendation. Perhaps the pastor will ask the council to reconsider a matter that he believes the council has overlooked. The council's disagreement may help him to see that some parishioners will doubt and even question his decision. But it is worth recalling that the council has a consultative-only vote and is not a deliberative or decision-making structure. If the council has responsibly discharged its threefold obligation of investigating, reflecting, and recommending its conclusions, then its work is done. The pastor has the freedom to accept or reject the council's advice. The Church does not oblige him to accept recommendations that he believes unwise.

The pastor who consults the council has good reason to see the council succeed. He should help the council to understand why he is consulting and the kind of recommendations he seeks. He should explain what kind of investigation will best serve the parish and how he intends to apply its results. When the council achieves a sound conclusion, the pastor should formally acknowledge the members' service. He may even explain to the parish as a whole that he has reached a decision after consultation with the council. This will build up the council's morale. It will also help the parish to understand what the council does and motivate people to offer their services to the council when an opening arises.

8: The Process for Pastoral Planning

Members of the parish pastoral council give their help in fostering pastoral activity by investigating, pondering and recommending their conclusions to the pastor. In Chapter Four we described this threefold function as pastoral planning. The term planning distinguishes the consultative process of the council from the executive or administrative functions of the pastor.

In Chapter Seven we described the operation of the council. By its research and reflection, we said, it lays the foundation for wise decisions by pastors. Pastors have the final say, but wise ones consult before deciding. They want their decisions on behalf of the parish to be prudent. The council does its work in close cooperation with the pastor. By consulting the council, he gives it a share in his ministry of leadership.

Chapter Eight is about the process of the council, that is, the series of steps that leads from a general consideration of an issue to a final decision by the pastor. In this chapter we will first examine the steps taken by the pastoral council under the rubric of "shared responsibility." The council does not have the responsibility for making choices on behalf of the parish, but it shares responsibility for investigating challenges faced by the parish and developing responses to them.

After looking at the steps taken by the council, we will examine the notion of process in general. We said that the pastor consults the council, asking it to study and reflect on a particular issue. As the pastoral council does its work, it may uncover aspects of an issue not foreseen by the pastor. He may ask the council to change course, turning its attention to the issues that have just emerged.

Shared Responsibility

Pastors consult councils in order to benefit from their advice. The terminus of the council's threefold work of investigating, reflecting, and recommending is a decision, made by the pastor on behalf of his people. Wise pastors may decide to follow council recommendations if they will strengthen the parish's mission and build up the community.

When councils first began in the late 1960s, however, many people looked at them skeptically. What good is a council that makes recommendations if the pastor may reject them? Isn't a consultative-only council merely the semblance of co-responsibility without any substance?

Such skepticism challenged pastors and council members to think more deeply about shared responsibility and about the relationship between the consultative pastor and the parish community. Clearly the church did not want to adopt a congregational type of polity and yield to parishioners the responsibility for parish governance. The church wanted to preserve its emphasis on the parish priest as the good shepherd. But it had to make explicit the teaching about the good shepherd and his knowledge of the flock. He and his parishioners are meant to form a communion. He calls them by name. He leads them to good pasture. He respects their gifts.

The church elaborated the consequences of the relationship between shepherd and flock as "shared responsibility." Shared responsibility differs from congregational polity, where congregants bear ultimate responsibility for church decision-making. In Catholic churches, by contrast, parishioners "share" responsibility. In other words, the pastor remains the official representative of the parish who speaks authoritatively on its behalf. Parishioners share responsibility by contributing to the governance of the church according to their talents and abilities. The pastor who is a good shepherd recognizes his community's gifts. He calls upon them to strengthen the parish.

This implies that pastors should have a particular skill, namely, the capacity for leading parish administration (Ippolito, 8). Such leadership entails a number of priestly abilities, such as the oversight of planning, implementation of new initiatives, the leadership of councils, the animation of the community, and being a good steward. But we can situate all of them under the rubric of sharing responsibility. The pastor who is a good shepherd consults his people because he knows and respects them. In them he has encountered God's Spirit.

Stages in Sharing Responsibility

Shared responsibility is a subtle concept because the pastor who "shares" responsibility does not "surrender" responsibility. He invites council members into the process of pastoral planning, but does not offer them the final choice. The pastor retains sole responsibility for that choice, and cannot delegate it to anyone else. Making the final choice is not, however, the only element in decision-making. The process involves many other elements, such as information-gathering, reflection, and the generation of options. With regard to those elements, the pastor enables the council to fully play its part.

Recognizing the diverse elements in decision-making is the key to shared responsibility. "The making of a choice is only one element in decision-making," wrote the canonist Robert T. Kennedy. Decision-making is complex, he said, and "involves several stages, only one of which is the making of a choice, and all of which entail the exercise of influence and power" (Kennedy, 9). Council members genuinely exercise power through their investigation, analysis, and recommendations. The power stems from their gifts and talents. The pastor who is a genuinely good shepherd recognizes them and builds upon them.

Let us consider the first of the pastoral council's responsibilities, that of investigation. The pastor has invited the council to examine a particular issue. It may be to reconsider the mission of the parish, or to make it more hospitable, or to create a pre-kindergarten for the elementary school, or to develop a policy for using parish facilities. The good pastor will give the council scope to investigate as thoroughly as possible.

Why is this so desirable? First of all, experienced pastors know our human propensity to assume as fact what we wish to be the case. We tend to see things as given and unchangeable which are only conditional and temporary. Pastors may curb this propensity by asking council members to study a matter impartially. "In the administrative life of the Church, no less than in the judicial, improved instruments are needed to ascertain facts accurately and thoroughly, and consistent efforts should be made to involve research-oriented and fact-oriented people in ecclesial problem-solving, program planning, and policy making" (Kennedy, 13). The pastoral council is just such an instrument. When the pastor asks it to thoroughly investigate, he avoids making false assumptions about what is true.

Consider also the council's second responsibility, pondering what it has investigated. This is perhaps the most creative step in the work of the pastoral council. The pastor himself may have already looked at the facts of the matter and drawn a conclusion. By doing so, he has seen as far into the matter as he is able to do. But the wise pastor recognizes that his abilities are limited. Like Socrates, he knows that he doesn't know everything. So he calls upon the pastoral council. Its members may be able to see something that the pastor did not see. One of the members may have an idea that is far-fetched but which, after being considered by other councilors, initiates a break-through in thinking. Properly developed, the idea may unite the community and advance its mission. The pastor does not need to be a creative genius to recognize the insight of others and harness it for the sake of the parish.

The council's third responsibility is to reach a conclusion and recommend it to the pastor. This appears to be simple – to conclude and recommend. But this third responsibility is more complicated than it seems, and introduces a temporal element into the process of the council.

The Temporal Element

Whenever we state that the pastoral council investigates, reflects, and finally recommends its conclusions, we may seem to imply that, with the recommendation, its work has come to an end. The process is seemingly complete. The council has submitted its conclusions to the pastor. He has the final choice to accept the recommendations or not. The council is not normally an implementing or executive body. So the recommendation apparently finishes the council's job.

However, a pastor may ask the council to implement what it has recommended. This is often the case. But the council that implements is not, as we said in Chapter Four, functioning as a council. Councils are consultative only. When councils implement, they work not as council members, but as volunteers under the pastor's direction. The main work of the council is investigating, reflecting, and recommending. After accomplishing its three tasks, the council's formal work – at least at first glance – is over.

But it is not true to say that the council, having reached a conclusion and recommended it, will never treat the matter again. Undoubtedly the pastor is the final decision-maker, and he implements parish decisions through the parish staff and through volunteers, even volunteers from the council. But the implementation of a decision is never the end of the decision. Choosing to implement a decision is, at first, nothing more than an expression of the pastor's and the parish's intentions.

The good intentions expressed in a decision need to assume concrete form. Pastoral councils usually express their good intentions by defining general goals and more precise objectives. But after the pastor has accepted a recommendation, and begun to implement the objectives, he may have further questions. Pastors may want to consult about the success of the new initiative. "Implementation involves attention to detail, selection and deployment of personnel, allocation and coordination of duties, delegation of authority, effective communication, sensitivity to persons, and adaptation to changing or unforeseen circumstances" (Kennedy, 14-15). The implementation may be a great success or it may be fraught with problems. Achieving the objectives may not be as easy as it first seemed. Pastors may want to ask the council how successful the implementation actually was.

Theorists distinguish between "strategic" and "adaptive" planning. Strategic planning is the development of a plan for a predicted future. Adaptive planning assumes that "any useful plan would be one that continuously adapts" (Lundholm-Eades, 125). A strategic plan, once it is formally accepted, needs to be monitored. Pastors may invite their councils to evaluate a plan or initiative in light of what they originally intended. The initiative was supposed to unify the parish and help it to achieve its mission. But the implementation of the initiative may have fallen short of the pastor's and council's good intentions.

Evaluation by the council may bring this to light. "Until such evaluation is made, it is premature to consider a decision as 'final,' for considerable alteration, even total reconsideration, may be necessary" (Kennedy, 15). The parish is a dynamic place, and the pastor may ask the council to reconsider matters that it had studied earlier.

In short, the basic functions of the pastoral council are to investigate, reflect, and recommend its conclusions. But in the process of pastoral planning, completing that threefold responsibility may not be the end of the council's involvement. Pastors may well ask the council to evaluate the implementation of an earlier recommendation. Such evaluation is another way in which the pastor shares responsibility.

PART TWO:
PARISH FINANCE COUNCILS

9. Theological Framework for Finance Councils

Parish, the Church Localized

Christ set up his Church on earth as a visible structure, a community of faith, hope, and love, and he sustains it unceasingly; through it he pours out grace and truth on everyone. This society, with its hierarchical structures, and the mystical body of Christ are one: a visible assembly and a spiritual community, an earthly Church and a Church enriched with heavenly gifts. It must not be considered as two things, but as forming one complex reality comprising human and divine elements. By analogy, the Church is like the mystery of the Word incarnate. Just as the assumed human nature of Christ serves the divine Word as a living instrument of salvation inseparably joined with him, in a similar way the social structure of the Church serves the Spirit of Christ who vivifies the Church toward the growth of the body of Christ. The Church needs human resources to carry out its mission. (Second Vatican Council, *Dogmatic Constitution on the Church* [1964], n. 8)

The parish is the local embodiment of the Church universal. The *Code of Canon Law* defines the parish as a community of the Christian faithful:

> A parish is a certain community of the Christian faithful stably constituted in a particular church (diocese), whose pastoral care is entrusted to a pastor ... under the authority of the diocesan bishop (c. 515 §1).
>
> A legitimately erected parish possesses juridical personality by the law itself (c. 515 §3).

The ecclesial community finds its most immediate and visible expression in the parish. It is the Church living in the midst of its sons and daughters. The parish is where Catholics know one another, worship together, are initiated into the community by baptism, confirmation, and Holy Eucharist, are formed in faith, and assist one another in many ways. It is the Church at its most real, the Church placed in the neighborhoods of humanity.

The Christian Faithful: Called and Empowered

Those baptized Christians, the ordinary members of the People of God, are referred to in the code as the "Christian faithful." They have been called the "protagonists" or "principal characters" of the 1983 *Code of Canon Law*; the previous code, in contrast, was envisioned as a handbook for the clergy. (It was published in Latin, and could not officially be translated into other languages.) The first canons in the section of the 1983 Code dedicated to "The Christian Faithful" define them this way:

> The Christian faithful are those who, inasmuch as they have been incorporated in Christ through baptism, have been constituted as the people of God. For this reason, made sharers in their own way in Christ's priestly, prophetic and royal function, they are called to exercise the mission which God has entrusted to the Church to fulfill in the world, in accord with the condition proper to each (c. 204 §1).

> Those baptized are fully in the communion of the Catholic Church on this earth who are joined with Christ in its visible structure by the bonds of the profession of faith, the sacraments, and ecclesiastical governance (c. 205).

These two terse canonical statements epitomize the rich and extensive theological teachings on "The People of God" in the *Dogmatic Constitution on the Church* (nn. 9-17) of the Second Vatican Council. They situate the fully incorporated members of the Church, lay persons, religious, and clergy, all together, as those called and empowered to actively participate in and take responsibility for the Church and its activities in mission.

Beneath this canonico-theological vision lies the presence and activity of the Church's Chief Protagonist, the Holy Spirit. Ultimately, the person and actions of the Spirit are what give life and grace and individual gifts to the believing faithful.

> ... the Holy Spirit not only sanctifies and guides the people of God by means of the sacraments and the ministries and adorns it with virtues, he also apportions his gifts "to each individually as he wills" (1 Cor 12:11), and among the faithful of every rank he distributes special graces

by which he renders them fit and ready to undertake the various offices which help the renewal and building up of the Church, according to that word: "To each is given the manifestation of the Spirit for the common good" (1 Cor 12:7). These charismatic gifts, whether they are very outstanding or simpler and more widely diffused, are to be accepted with thanksgiving and consolation, since they are primarily suited to and useful for the needs of the Church (*Dogmatic Constitution on the Church*, n. 12).

The gifts and graces of the Holy Spirit are intermingled with the natural talents, education, and experience of individual persons, and often the gifts are not entirely distinguishable from them. These individuals, fully incorporated into the Church, with their abilities and gifts, are both called and empowered to play their role within the Church and outside it in the world.

A Church That Goes Forth

Pope Francis, in his visionary apostolic exhortation, *The Joy of the Gospel* (2013) called the Church to heed the direction that the Risen Christ gave to his disciples, "Go forth and make disciples of all nations, ... teaching them to observe all that I have commanded you" (Mt 28:19-20). In the section entitled "The Church's Missionary Transformation," the pope called the Church to conversion and renewal, to reach out, to become "a Church that goes forth."

> The church that "goes forth" is a community of missionary disciples who take the first step, who are involved and supportive, who bear fruit and rejoice. An evangelizing community knows that the Lord has taken the initiative, he has loved us first (cf. 1 Jn 4:19), and therefore we can move forward, boldly take the initiative, go out to others, seek those who have fallen away, stand at the crossroads and welcome the outcast (n. 24).

Such a community desires to show mercy and to be involved in people's daily lives. It supports and stands by people at every step of the way because the Lord wants it to be fruitful. It is filled with joy and knows how to rejoice always. The community evangelizes and is itself evangelized through the beauty of the liturgy, which is both a celebration of the task of evangelization and the source of its renewed self-giving.

> The parish is not an outdated institution; precisely because it possesses great flexibility, it can assume quite different contours depending on the openness and missionary creativity of the pastor and the community. . . . if it proves capable of self-renewal and constant adaptivity, it continues to be "the church living in the midst of the homes of its sons and daughters."
>
> This presumes that it really is in contact with the homes and the lives of its people, and does not become a useless structure out of touch with people or a self-absorbed cluster made up of a chosen few. The parish is the presence of the church in a given territory, an environment for hearing God's word, for growth in the Christian life, for dialogue, proclamation, charitable outreach, worship, and celebration. . . . It is a community of communities, a sanctuary where the thirsty come to drink in the midst of their journey and a center of constant missionary outreach. (n. 28).

Pope Francis goes on to point out the role of the Holy Spirit in the evangelizing Church. The Spirit enriches the Church with different charisms. These gifts are meant to renew and build up the Church. They are not an inheritance, safely secured and entrusted to a small group for safe-keeping; rather they are gifts of the Spirit integrated into the body of the Church . . . and then channeled into an evangelizing impulse. "A sure sign of the authenticity of a charism is its ecclesial character, its ability to be integrated harmoniously into the life of God's holy and faithful people for the good of all" (n. 130).

Structures of Participation

In *The Joy of the Gospel* Pope Francis spoke of pastoral activity, conversion, and ecclesial renewal that cannot not be deferred. In that context, he referred explicitly to the "means of participation" in the *Code of Canon Law*, which specifically include parish pastoral councils and parish finance councils. These should be encouraged and developed as one way of "fostering a dynamic, open and missionary communion." These and other forms of pastoral dialogue should spring from a desire to listen to everyone, and not simply those who would tell pastors what they would like to hear. "[T]he principal aim of these participatory processes should not be ecclesiastical organization, but rather the missionary aspiration of reaching everyone" (n. 31).

The canonical system has long employed "participatory structures" or "consultative bodies" whereby the Christian faithful share in the leadership and decision-making at every level of the Church's life. One reason for the existence of these structures is practical, that is, to provide some transparency to policies and decisions, to avoid rash or foolish judgments, and to prevent criminal activity; but the more radical reasons are the responsibilities of all the baptized and their access to the Holy Spirit's guidance.

Pope Francis reminds us of the responsibility that comes with our baptism.

> In virtue of their baptism, all the members of the People of God have become missionary disciples (Mt 28:19). All the baptized, whatever their position in the Church or their level of instruction in the faith, are agents of evangelization, and it would be insufficient to envisage a plan of evangelization to be carried out by professionals, while the rest of the faithful would simply be passive recipients. The new evangelization calls for personal involvement on the part of each of the baptized. Every Christian is challenged, here and now, to be actively engaged in evangelization; indeed, anyone who has truly experienced God's saving love does not need much time or lengthy training to go out and proclaim that love (*The Joy of the Gospel*, n. 120).

The passage from the *Dogmatic Constitution on the Church*, n. 12, quoted above, specifies the various ways that the Holy Spirit sanctifies and guides the Church. Each one of the Christian faithful possesses the Spirit of Christ (n. 14), and is able to give voice to the Spirit. It isn't only bishops and pastors who receive the gifts of the Spirit, it is every one of the faithful. One of the places for speaking and listening for the Spirit is in the local "structure of participation," the parish finance council.

The 1983 *Code of Canon Law* states that the purpose of the parish finance council is "to assist the pastor in the administration of the goods of the parish" (c. 537). This statement of purpose might lead some to think that the principal role of the parish finance council is to safeguard the parish assets and protect them from dissipation, destruction, or theft. But Pope Francis in *The Joy of the Gospel* hints at a broader prospect:

> I hope that all communities will devote the necessary effort to advancing along the path of pastoral and missionary conversion that cannot leave things as they presently are. "Mere administration" can no longer be enough. Throughout the world, let us be "permanently in a state of mission" (n. 25).
>
> I dream of a "missionary option," that is, a missionary impulse capable of transforming everything, so that the Church's customs, ways of doing things, times and schedules, language and structures can be suitably channeled for the evangelization of today's world rather than for self-preservation (n. 27).

This is a challenge to do more than "mere maintenance" or "business as usual."

10: Canonical Framework for Finance Councils

Canon 537 of the 1983 *Code of Canon Law* calls for a finance council in every Catholic parish:

> In each parish there is to be a finance council which is governed, in addition to universal law, by norms issued by the diocesan bishop and in which the Christian faithful, selected according to these same norms, are to assist the pastor in the administration of the goods of the parish, without prejudice to the prescript of canon 532.

Canon 532 (*CCEO* c. 290 §1) asserts that the pastor is the agent for the parish in all legal matters:

> In all juridic affairs the pastor represents the parish according to the norm of law. He is to take care that the goods of the parish are administered according to the norms of canons 1281-1288.

These canons, 1281-1288, located in the code's Book V, "The Temporal Goods of the Church," Title II, "The Administration of Goods," stipulate in considerable detail the duties of administrators of church property. The corresponding canons in the *Code of Canons of the Eastern Churches* are 1022-1033. These canons set forth rules for borrowing money, paying off debts, protecting the property with insurance, preparing budgets of income and expenditures, keeping well organized books, drawing up an annual report, paying employees just wages, and much more.

In addition to the canons of the *Code of Canon Law*, which are the rules for the Church universal, each diocese has its own particular norms, policies, or guidelines for the administration of monies, properties, and furnishings. These are also "canon law," and oblige every church administrator and every parish in the diocese.

In initial summary, then, the pastor is the administrator of the goods of the parish, and the finance council is to assist him in the fulfillment of that task.

The Purpose of the Finance Council

Parishes are described in canon law as stably constituted communities of the Christian faithful whose pastoral care is entrusted to a pastor under the authority of the diocesan bishop. Parishes exist for religious purposes, to carry on the mission which God has entrusted to the church in the world. In order to fulfill that religious mission, parishes must make use of "temporal goods."

"Temporal goods" is the canonical description for the non-spiritual assets, tangible and intangible, that the Church uses to carry out its work: land, buildings, furnishings, money, vehicles, securities, and other kinds of real or personal property. In the parish context, it refers to the goods that belong to the parish, not to the things that are the personal property of the pastor or other church personnel. Each parish is a juridic person, that is, it has legal personality, standing in canon law – and often in civil law as well. It is the property of the parish as a legally recognized person that constitutes its "temporal goods."

In the canonical system all juridic persons, e.g., parishes, dioceses, seminaries, religious communities, are required to have a finance council to assist their administrators to fulfill their function. The parish pastor is the administrator of the temporal goods of the parish, and like all other juridic persons, the parish has a finance council to assist him in that task.

The purpose of the parish finance council is not to oversee or "second guess" the pastor in his role as administrator. The pastor is presumed to be honest and truthful, after all, bishops have vouched for his moral integrity both at the time of his ordination and when he was appointed pastor (cc. 1029; 521 §2). However, the pastor may not possess great financial familiarity or business acumen; his years of training before ordination were not strongly focused on matters of management, though many pastors have acquired remarkable expertise as administrators.

The finance council is advisory to the pastor as administrator. It is not to serve as a substitute or replacement administrator. Its relationship to the pastor is collaborative, not a supervisory one. The pastor asks for advice and assistance, often technical information or expert insight, from the finance council, whose members have background, expertise, and experience in such matters. Even though final decisions are with the pastor, and he alone answers to the bishop's authority, the value of the finance council's role in the life and welfare of the parish is hard to overestimate. It is a stellar example of the kind of active participation and co-responsibility of laity in the life of the Church. Its members make crucial contributions to their own parish community.

Even though the finance council is advisory to the pastor, and not his supervisor, still its very existence and function serve as a form of "check and balance," by bringing its wisdom to bear on the financial affairs of the parish. The council, by performing its advise and review roles, gives the parish community assurance that its accounts are in good order and that its financial transactions, like contracts and purchases, are fair and above board.

Another form of "check and balance" is the annual report which the pastor is obliged to submit to the diocesan bishop, and the bishop, in turn is required to submit it for examination to his diocesan finance council (c. 1287 §1). The parish finance council should be involved in the preparation or review of this annual report.

The finance council, besides its primary concern with parish accounts and properties, also bears some responsibilities in the area of "human resources," that is, the employment and working conditions of parish employees. Canon 1286 (*CCEO* c. 1030) calls for administrators to observe civil laws on labor and social policy in addition to the Church's social teachings, and to pay employees just and decent wages.

A Parallel Structure: The Diocesan Finance Council

As was the case with parish pastoral councils, much can be learned about the purpose and configuration of parish finance councils by looking to the similar structure at the diocesan level, the diocesan finance council, outlined in canons 492 and 493 of the 1983 Code. They are analogous canonical structures, but the diocesan council is described in greater detail than the parish council; and it serves as "a parallel place" to consult when exploring the meaning of the canon on parish finance councils (see c. 17).

However, all of the details of the diocesan council need not be copied to fill in the blanks of the parish structure, since the former is presumed to have a much larger talent pool to draw from and much greater monetary and real property assets to monitor than a parish finance council. Plus, the diocese has a finance officer to administer the goods of the diocese under the authority of the bishop, while the parish pastor may not have that luxury (c. 494).

A reminder: the diocesan guidelines or policies for parish finance councils, issued by the bishop, are a primary source for how the councils are to be formed and to operate. Resort to the diocesan finance council as a parallel is strictly a secondary source.

Another source for guidance is the National Conference of Catholic Bishops Committee on Budget and Finance document, *Diocesan Internal Controls: A Framework*, issued in 1995 and available online at http://www.usccb.org/finance/internal.shtml.

The Eastern Catholic Churches

The Eastern Catholic Churches also have a requirement for a finance council in each parish. Canon 295 of the *Code of Canons of the Eastern Churches*, issued in 1990 by Pope John Paul II, calls for a council to deal with financial matters in every parish, in accord with the rules of each one of the autonomous Churches:

> In the parish there are to be appropriate councils dealing with pastoral and financial matters, in accord with the norms of the particular law of its own Church *sui iuris*.

The canon refers the matter of parish finance councils to the canonical regulations of each Eastern Church, but those rules could leave the details of the structures of the councils to the individual eparchial bishops.

11. ROOTS IN THE SECOND VATICAN COUNCIL AND OTHER DOCUMENTS

In contrast to the parish *pastoral* council, which is a creation of the Second Vatican Council, the parish *finance* council has a longer history. In the former *Code of Canon Law* (1917), and even before, in the mid-19th century, there were in many parishes a "council of the fabric of the church," or "council of administration," commonly called the "board of trustees." Its members were appointed by the bishop, and the council was in charge of "the proper administration of the goods of the church" (*CIC* 17, cc. 1183-1184). Still, its status was advisory to the pastor who was the administrator of the parish properties.

The third plenary council of Baltimore in 1884, which enacted policies and regulations for the Church in the United States, issued detailed guidelines for these councils. Each bishop was to judge whether such lay councils were necessary, and how their members were to be selected. He was to give approval to those persons proposed by the pastor for membership on the council. The parishioners chosen were to be over twenty-one years of age, have made their Easter duty, have contributed to the support of the parish, have their children in Catholic schools, and not hold membership in secret or forbidden societies. These regulations from the Council of Baltimore are no longer in force, but questions still arise about who can serve on today's parish finance councils.

Documents of the Second Vatican Council

The source for parish finance councils in the documents of the Second Vatican Council is found in the *Decree on the Ministry and Life of Priests* (1965):

> What is in the technical sense church property should be managed by priests, as its nature requires, according to church law and as far as possible with the help of expert laity. They should always apply it for the purposes for which it is permissible for the church to possess temporal goods, namely for the celebration of divine worship, for the reasonable maintenance of the clergy, and for carrying out the works of the apostolate and of charity, especially to the poor (n. 17).

The same *Decree* speaks of the attitude priests should have toward lay persons, which serves as a context for their collaboration in finance councils:

> Priests should sincerely acknowledge and promote the standing of the laity and their proper role in the church's mission. . . . They should readily listen to lay people, considering their wishes as those of sisters and brothers, recognizing their experience and competence in various fields of human activity, so as to join with them in reading the signs of the times. . . They should, then, confidently entrust responsibilities to the laity in the service of the church, giving them scope and freedom for action ... (n. 9).

These same attitudes toward lay persons and their contributions to the church's mission found their place in the 1983 *Code of Canon Law*. Pastors, as a part of their responsibilities, are urged to recognize and promote the proper part which lay persons have in the mission of the Church (c. 529 §2). And canon 228 §2 states: "Lay persons who excel in necessary knowledge, prudence, and integrity, are qualified to assist pastors of the Church as experts and advisors, even in councils, according to the norm of law."

The Vatican Council's *Decree on the Apostolate of the Laity* (1965) echoes and supports these forms of lay involvement within the Church:

> Sharing in Christ's priestly, prophetic, and kingly office, the laity have an active part to play in the church's life and work. Within Christian communities their activity is so necessary that without it the pastor's apostolate cannot generally attain its full effect ... by the offering of their own particular skills they make the care of souls and also the administration of the church's goods more effective (n.10).

Directory on the Pastoral Office of Bishops

After the Second Vatican Council the Congregation for Bishops issued a set of guidelines to assist bishops in their care of souls, it was called a *Directory on the Pastoral Office of Bishops* (1973). In the chapter on "The Bishop as Guardian of the Communion of Charity," it inserted a section on "Administration of Church Property" that begins with a paragraph entitled, "Participation of the Community in the Administration of Church Property":

> The bishop takes suitable measures that the faithful may be educated in a sense of participation and cooperation also as regards the temporal goods which the church needs to fulfill her purpose, so that all according to their individual capacities consider themselves co-responsible both in the economic support of the church community and of its works and charities, as well as in the preservation, increase and proper administration of the community's temporalities (n. 133).

Then the *Directory* goes on to speak of "Establishment of Councils for Administering Temporalities in the Diocese, in Parishes, and in Other Ecclesiastical Organizations":

> The bishop should see to the erection of councils in the diocese and also in every parish ... and on these councils he is to include laity, as far as possible, along with the clergy (*PO* 17) – laity selected from among men who have administrative ability, an upright character, and zeal for the apostolate of the Church (n. 135).

The Congregation for Bishops issued an updated version of the pastoral manual for bishops in 2004, the *Directory for the Pastoral Ministry of Bishops*. It offered little on parish finance councils, but it did say in its chapter on the parish that "The bishop regulates *parochial administration* with special reference to the following: ... Parish Finance Council. Regardless of the number of parishioners, every parish must have a finance council" (n. 210). And, when treating of the bishop's "procedure for a parish pastoral visit" (one of the bishop's many obligations), he should "have a meeting with the parish finance council" (n. 221).

Clearly parish finance councils continue to play a very significant role in the parish as a community of the Christian faithful.

Diocesan Norms

The norms issued by the diocesan bishop for finance councils are of more immediate and practical importance than most of the foregoing source documents. The policies and guidelines for the local diocese set forth the standards and expectations for parish finance councils, and should be made available to every member of every council. If these norms are not available or are in need of updating, that should be brought to the attention of the diocesan bishop.

National Conference of Catholic Bishops

The National Conference of Catholic Bishops Committee on Budget and Finance issued a document in 1995 entitled, *Diocesan Internal Controls: A Framework.* It is available at the website of the USCCB. This thorough and specific report, although targeted at the diocesan financial controls, offers guidance that may be helpful to parish finance councils.

The United States Conference of Catholic Bishops Ad Hoc Committee on Diocesan Audits presented a brief "Report to the Body of Bishops" in 2007. Available at the USCCB website, it is focused on internal audit procedures at the parish level, and includes the role of parish finance councils.

12: Functions of the Parish Finance Council

"To assist the pastor in the administration of the goods of the parish" – that is the function of the parish finance council as described in canon 537. The key words are "assist," "administration," and "goods." The verb "to assist" suggests a particular relationship between the council and the pastor. The council *assists* him because he (as the parish's official representative) remains ultimately responsible for the goods of the parish. In relation to him, the council has an ancillary and helping relationship. This relationship is essential, however, because the pastor and the council enjoy a community of interest and faith. The council assists the pastor because, rightly understood, he and they are united in a common Christian mission. In faith the members of the council put their talents at the service of the pastor and the parish. The pastor recognizes their value to his ministry and draws upon the members' expertise.

The council assists the pastor in a particular area, namely, the *administration* of the parish's *goods*. The word "administration" links the work of the council to ministerial service. The council serves by offering to the pastor its support and knowledge regarding the parish's "goods" or property. If the goods are to be well employed, they require the exercise of stewardship. Stewardship means, among other things, their preservation, increase, and proper use. In this sense, the stewardship of parish goods is very much akin to stewardship in general. Pastors can learn from the practices of expert administrators in the secular world.

But the stewardship of parish goods may differ from administration in other realms. Church stewardship differs because the mission of the church differs. The stewards of parish goods put them at the service of the Church's mission. That mission may require adjustments to stewardship as it is understood in the secular world. Church administration does not seek the preservation and increase of parish goods unreflectively and in routine fashion. Rather it preserves and increases them – or it spends and decreases them – for the sake of the Christian mission. Stewardship may take different forms, depending on the call of the gospel.

In this chapter we will see first how the parish finance council functions in the service of sound administration in general. It helps the pastor exercise his administrative responsibilities as would any good steward of resources. Then we will see how the finance council, as a consultative body, shares responsibility with the pastor for the goods of the parish.

This may create tensions within the finance council regarding administration and stewardship. But the recognition of such tensions, and dialogue about them, are also part of the function of the finance council.

Sound Administration in General

The recommendations of the parish finance council should reflect the best practices of administration in general. In Chapter Fifteen, we shall review actual best practices by today's finance councils. For the present, it is enough to see that the function of every finance council is to advise the pastor to adopt the administrative norms and practices of excellent institutions throughout society. Although the pastor is "steward for the parish mission" (Peri, 16), nevertheless he calls upon the help of those for whom stewardship is a secular vocation, including those who know how to manage things efficiently, how to report finances reliably, and how to comply with laws and regulations. The typical priest-pastor has had little training in management and needs the skills of the trained manager if he is to minimize risks to the parish's mission. "Risk management forces us to step outside our comfort zone and think like lawyers, accountants, businessmen, insurance agents, contractors, and more" (McGovern, 63). These professionals may be outside the comfort zone of many pastors, but they have skills that parishes need.

Fiscal Standards. The U.S. Bishops have stated that good stewardship of parish resources "must include the most stringent ethical, legal, and fiscal standards" (USCCB [2002], 32). Let us look at each of these, beginning with the fiscal standards. In many dioceses, the primary responsibility of the finance council is to review the parish's annual budget. The first step in preparing the budget is to study the income reports for the recent past (e.g., the past five years). The more detailed the reports, the more reliably the pastor can calculate trends so as to estimate the coming year's income. Once the estimate is made, the pastor (with his advisors and staff) should commit the parish to it as a spending cap. The estimate represents the best guess about next year's income.

The estimate, however, is only the first step in budgeting. The second step is to plan how to spend the hoped-for income. Experts in budgeting say that this planning ought to be a months-long process of discernment and negotiation. "By operating in this fashion, the managers and employees who are involved in the budget process will feel more a part of the management of resources than if a budget were imposed on them."

(Thompson, 253). The annual budget is the dollar cost of achieving the parish mission for one year. People will differ on how best to achieve that mission. A process of discernment and negotiation will enable the pastor to make a prudent decision based on the shared wisdom of this staff and advisors, and identify places where he can reduce spending if needed.

To be sure, there are areas in the budget where the pastor has relatively little discretionary room in cutting expenses. It is not easy to reduce the parish payroll, for example, without eliminating employees. Moreover, every parish has fixed expenses – for example, insurance fees, loan repayments, and diocesan assessments – to which it is already committed. On top of these expenses, the prudent pastor will contribute a portion of parish income to future capital expenses, such as painting and re-roofing. He can undoubtedly reduce his capital budget when faced with a shortfall, but he does so at the parish's long-term risk. The only places where pastors can readily tighten the parish's belt are in terms of day-to-day operating costs and discretionary spending for ministry. Comprehensive and accurate spending records will facilitate the reconciliation of the parish's actual income with expenses. In making fiscal judgments, a pastor will consult his finance council. He wants to adhere, when making and reconciling the budget, to the fiscal standards recommended by experts. This will also enable him to confidently and transparently report on the budget to parishioners.

Ethical Standards. Having looked briefly at fiscal standards, let us turn to ethical standards as the professional rules of conduct to which parish administration should conform. In 2007, the U.S. Bishops considered how the use of parish audits would enhance the transparency and accountability of Church finances and wise stewardship by pastors and administrators. The bishops concluded that such audits "would help ensure parishes are following appropriate business practices, civil regulation and diocesan requirements and procedures" (USCCB [2007], 2). An audit is the examination of records with the intent to verify them and correct problems that may arise.

One of the advantages of an external audit is the professionalism of the auditor. Such audits are typically completed by "a certified public accountant (CPA) who has completed a required degree program, passed a rigorous licensing exam, and worked for a period of time performing certified audits under the supervision of a CPA" (Thompson, 244). If an external audit is not required by the diocese, finance councils can oversee an internal audit conducted by the parish bookkeeper. This will help the pastor ascertain whether parish record keeping, accounting and reporting comply with professional standards and diocesan policies.

<u>Legal Standards</u>. Finally let us turn to the parish's legal standards, about which the finance council also advises the pastor. Compliance with the civil law is a complicated matter compounded by the fact that the legal status of a parish may differ from state to state. In some states, the diocese itself is a single corporation, to which individual parishes belong and for which the diocese is the responsible legal entity. In other states, individual parishes are civil corporations with their own board of directors and corporate duties (Dantuono, 214-216). Although the finance council is a requirement of canon law, not civil law, its members should have a broad knowledge of the civil responsibilities of the pastor. The finance council should help him to act on behalf of the parish in a reasonable and informed manner. It should advise him to see what is in the parish's best interest. It should recommend how he can carry out the parish's mission in accord with civil law.

Experts in the law have identified a number of areas in which the Catholic parish and parochial school are vulnerable to legal action. Negligence, experts tell us, is the most often-litigated tort or wrongful injury (Shaughnessy, 98). When Catholic institutions violate their duty to provide a safe environment and an injury occurs, the parish may have to compensate the injured party. In addition to negligence, contracts provide another occasion for possible legal action. Contracts govern the relation between the parish and its employees, between the parochial school and the children it enrolls, and between religious education volunteers and those whom they catechize. The parish relates to vendors, suppliers, and maintenance services by means of contracts. The finance council can advise pastors about them, as well as about employment practices, parochial school handbooks, and the rules and procedures governing parish volunteers. If the parish is to conform to the highest legal standards, the pastor should heed advisors who know the application of the law in the parochial setting.

The finance council functions, in short, to help pastors adhere to the standards of administration practiced by excellent institutions throughout society. Pastors who adopt these standards are better stewards. When parishes follow stringent fiscal, ethical and legal practices, they are better able to shed the light of the Gospel upon society.

Shared Responsibility in the Finance Council

The finance council, we recall, plays a consultative role. It assists the pastor who is accountable to the bishop for the stewardship and administration of the parish's temporal goods. Because the finance council is consultative, and does not have decision-making authority, one might be tempted to think that it shares little responsibility, since the pastor is not obliged to accept its advice.

But the U.S. Bishops do not view the finance council's responsibility in this light. The 2009 document by the U.S. Bishops, entitled *Diocesan Financial Issues*, includes a 20-page section on "Parish Financial Management" (USCCB [2009], section I-I). The section features an adaptation of the 2007 "Parish Finance Council Guidelines" of the Archdiocese of Chicago. The finance council guidelines clarify the bishops' attitude toward the responsibility that the pastor shares with the council.

First of all, the bishops understand the finance council as enhancing the pastor's ability to be accountable to his diocesan bishop. They write, "An active, well-formed Parish Finance Council is a key element for promoting the financial health of a parish, assuring accountability and assisting the pastor with his temporal responsibilities" (USCCB [2009], 8). By engaging with the pastor in a dialogue about the goods of the parish, the finance council clarifies the pastor's thought about his temporal responsibilities, enabling him to render the bishop a good account of them.

The finance council, second of all, is to be "active" and well-formed." That falls in large part to the pastor. The bishops affirm that the pastor has the responsibility "to give the members [of the finance council] appropriate background and enrichment so they are able to carry out their duties" (USCCB [2009], 9). Such background and enrichment will include the information needed to accurately understand the parish's financial situation. To be sure, the pastor consults the council and is not obliged to accept the finance council's advice. But at the same time, he has to enable the council to do its duty. He has to help them to help him.

Finally, the bishops make it clear that the pastor is to take the advice of the council seriously. Although the finance council does not have decision-making authority, nevertheless "The pastor should not act against such advice [i.e., the recommendations offered by the finance council], especially when there is consensus, unless there is an overriding reason" (USCCB [2009], 9). Consultation, the bishops say, is at the heart of the decision-making process. Developing consensus is part of that process. And when such consensus exists among the finance council members, the pastor should normally accept their advice.

Service on the finance council expresses a genuine Christian spirituality. The finance council member assimilates the mission of Christ within a specifically ecclesial response to God's Word. The administration of the parish's goods is closely linked to the parish's mission. "The budget is a moral as well as a financial document as it reveals the values and priorities of the organization" (Thompson, 237), that is, the parish. By advising the pastor on the parish budget, the finance council helps him to see that receiving parish donations and spending them wisely contributes to achieving the mission of Christ and the church.

Every finance council occasionally witnesses a dispute about how best to accomplish the parish's mission. Some members may feel, for example, that the mission is best served by an act of generous sacrifice of parish resources on behalf of the poor. Others may feel that stewardship requires disciplined saving for long-term needs. Such disagreements do not represent a failure of consensus on the part of council members. Quite likely the disagreements serve the function of the finance council in an exemplary way. A spirited give-and-take can help the pastor to recognize the values involved in the parish's financial decisions.

The Catholic parish, like every other organization in society with financial commitments, dedicates itself to achieving a specific mission. In achieving this mission, it should strive for the highest ethical, legal, and fiscal standards. The finance council functions by bringing these standards to the attention of the pastor and helping him apply them to the administration of the parish's goods.

13: PARISH FINANCE COUNCIL RELATIONSHIPS

This chapter on parish finance council relationships begins with the same distinction that we made in Chapter Five regarding parish pastoral council relationships. The finance council, like the pastoral council, relates primarily to the pastor. He consults the finance council about the administration of parish goods. The council advises him. That is its primary relationship. In addition to this primary relationship, the finance council has secondary relationships. It relates to the parish staff (especially the parish business manager or bookkeeper), to the pastoral council, and to parishioners at large. But these are not primary relationships. These other groups do not usually consult the finance council. Consultation belongs mainly to the pastor.

When he consults the finance council, the pastor is looking for assistance. We have already seen the three main areas in which the pastor may seek advice:

- The evaluation and review of parish financial statements,
- Parish managerial decision-making extending beyond financial statements, and
- The oversight of parish financial controls.

Just as the pastor looks for the pastoral council's help in investigating, reflecting, and recommending conclusions about general and practical parish matters, so he looks for the finance council's help in advising him about the administration of parish goods, especially finances.

So the distinction between primary and secondary relationships holds true for the finance council, just as it does for the pastoral council. But as this chapter will show, there are important differences in the relationships between the pastor and the two councils. We shall begin with the differences in the type of knowledge that the two councils seek, differences important to pastor-council relationships. We shall also see the pastor's relationship of cooperation with the parish finance council. He cooperates, or shares responsibility, with the council when he chooses to rely upon its good judgment in financial and other administrative matters. Finally, we shall summarize the secondary relationships that the finance council has with the parish staff, the pastoral council, and parishioners at large.

Types of Knowledge

It is important to distinguish between the kind of knowledge that the pastor seeks from the pastoral and the finance council, because the distinction has consequences for the relationship between the pastor and his councils. First, from the pastoral council, the pastor seeks recommendations about action that is wise and prudent. In other words, he consults the council about what to do in a particular situation. It is not the kind of answer that one can necessarily find in a textbook. The situation depends on many variables, such as the faith and morale of the congregation, and the issues that the parish faces. The pastor consults the pastoral council because the wise and prudent course of action will change according to the situation of the parish, and the nature of problem to be addressed.

From the parish finance council, in the second place, the pastor seeks a specialized kind of knowledge. It is not primarily the wise and prudent knowledge of how to act in a changing situation. It is rather the technical knowledge that belongs to experts in a variety of fields: financial knowledge, administrative knowledge, and legal knowledge. The pastor consults the finance council, not because he needs to discuss what is prudent in general, but because he needs expertise. It is the expert knowledge of people who know the standards of business: evaluating income and expenses, weighing decisions in the light of civil law, and controlling finances.

This has consequences for the relationship between the pastor and the finance council members. In the pastoral council, the pastor and the members seek a kind of wisdom about which no one is an expert. It is the wisdom of what to do in a changing situation. It may require a gradual discernment. But in the finance council, the pastor consults people who may know more than he does about finance, administration, and business. Ideally, the finance council members have had expert training in fields such as accounting and law. The pastor consults them as one might consult a professional in a field other than one's own. He assumes that they are committed to the parish, and will dedicate their skills to the parish's well-being. He should be pre-disposed to accept their recommendations.

Relationships of Cooperation

The pastor consults the finance council as one consults experts, but he may not surrender to the finance council his responsibility for the overall well-being of the parish, including its administration. His relation to the council is complex. It is difficult to define how the pastor shares responsibility without surrendering it. Some authors have said that the pastor leads and governs, but need not manage (Lundholm-Eades, 36; Wall, 97). According to this viewpoint, the pastor has to exercise general oversight, but need not attend to every administrative detail. Much of parish management can be left to a business manager after consultation with the finance council.

The wise choice to leave minor decisions to others, however, presupposes an experienced pastor. He ought to have a Socratic insight into the limits of his knowledge. He need not be an expert in finance, law, or human resources. But he does need to know "enough about these complex areas to make sure they're being efficiently managed" (Brough, 113). That knowledge comes with experience. The wise pastor must be humble enough to acknowledge that he lacks expertise, but shrewd enough to identify trustworthy councillors upon whose judgment he can rely.

In professional relationships, such as the one that should exist between the pastor and the finance council, council members should avoid conflicts of interest. The U.S. Bishops have called attention to the potential for such conflicts that threaten the loyalty of the council member to the parish. They recommend that council members should regularly disclose private interests that may conflict with the parish's interests.

> On an annual basis the parish Finance Council members should disclose in writing any known financial interest that the individual, or a member of the individual's family, has in any business entity that transacts business with the parish (USCCB [2009], I-I-13).

The wise pastor knows that conflicts of interest may arise. He asks the finance council members to acknowledge conflicts and disclose them publically.

Secondary Relationships

In addition to its primary relationship with the pastor, the finance council has secondary relationships with the parish business manager and other staff members, the pastoral council, and the parish at large.

Parish Staff. In order to do its work, the finance council must have access to the parish's charts of financial accounts. For example, the council needs to review the records of past contributions to the parish in order to estimate the income for the next year. Or to give another example, the council needs to compare the amounts budgeted for various parish spending categories in the past in order to assess changes in spending categories for the future. This requires a good working relationship with the parish bookkeeper or business manager. The U.S. Bishops recommend that parish employees should give to the finance council "relevant and timely information including financial reports" (USCCB [2009], I-I-13).

The U.S. Bishops also recommended in the same place that parish employees should *not* be members of the finance council. The parish business manager or bookkeeper should attend meetings, they say, but in a consultative, non-voting capacity. A 2007 survey of parishes revealed that this is often the case. In the 53 percent of parishes that have a business manager, the business manager is a nonvoting member 57 percent of the time (Zech [2010], 64).

Pastoral Council. The U.S. Bishops have recommended that finance councils have a good working relationship with the pastoral council, but should not be a part of the pastoral council structure (USCCB [2009], I-I-16). In actual practice, however, it is somewhat common for a member of the finance council to sit on the pastoral council. The 2007 survey reported that 39 percent of pastoral councils have at least one voting member who sits on the finance council, and an additional 14 percent have a non-voting ex officio member from the finance council (Zech [2010], 92). The two councils commonly have this kind of relationship.

Having said that, it remains true that the finance council, with its focus on the administration of parish goods, is separate from the pastoral council. The pastor consults the finance council for expert advice on financial statements, administrative decisions, and financial controls. He consults the pastoral council for prudent advice but not necessarily expert opinion. He may invite a member of one council to inform the members of the other council, but a formal relationship between the two is not required.

The general principle is that the pastor will consult as he deems it necessary or as the law requires. The finance council focuses on administration of parish goods. The pastoral council focuses on matters having to do with pastoral leadership. As we shall see in Chapter Fifteen, many pastors draft their budget in consultation with the finance council, and then present it to the pastoral council for feedback. The two councils may need to communicate, but one is not superior to the other.

Parishioners. The finance council has a secondary relationship with parishioners who have a general interest in the parish's financial situation. They want to know that the pastor is a good steward of their financial contributions. They deserve to know when the parish encounters financial problems.

The finance council, in evaluating and reviewing parish financial statements and in overseeing financial controls, needs to have accurate knowledge of the parish. When questions arise, members should be able to speak to the parties responsible. These include parish committees, organizations, project leaders and ministries. They in turn need to know about the finance council and the role it plays. Parishioners should know that the finance council advises the pastor on the parish's finances and that it plays a role in ensuring the good stewardship of parish resources. The finance council's knowledge of the parish, and the parishioners' knowledge of the council, work to the benefit of all.

Usually the parish finance council plays a role in preparing an annual financial report to the parish. This annual report allows the pastor to manifest his care for the parish's goods. The parish report should be more than a record of total annual income and total expense. One expert (Thompson, 243) has recommended that the report should include a balance sheet, a statement of activities, and a cash flow statement:

- The balance sheet will show all of the parish's material assets (including the value of its real estate and buildings) as well as the total amount the parish owes to its creditors.

- The statement of activities will show how much income the parish collected (including what it earned from its investments) and how much the parish paid in annual expenses (including what it paid on its loans).

- The cash flow statement will explain how much was moved from the bank (financing) and spent on construction (investing in the parish plant).

An annual financial report to the parish with this three-part structure would give parishioners an accurate snapshot of the parish's fiscal health. By helping to prepare such a statement, the finance council would show the pastor's good stewardship for the parish resources.

Shared Responsibility with the Finance Council

We began this chapter by noting a difference in the way that the pastor relates to the finance council. Unlike the pastoral council – whose members are not experts but who contribute their practical wisdom and prudent advice – the finance council is made up of experts. The pastor consults them as one might consult a doctor or lawyer. The wise pastor knows the limits of his knowledge. He does not usually have the skills of a bookkeeper, legal professional, or business owner. But he must be shrewd enough to gauge the quality of their advice and confident enough to trust it. Having chosen his council members, he will be disposed to accept their advice. Although some authors argue that the pastor "leads" and "governs" but does not "manage," nevertheless he remains the parish's chief steward. He is ultimately responsible for the administration of its goods. The pastor shares responsibility with the finance council, just as he does with the pastoral council and the parish staff, but he cannot surrender that responsibility. Because he consults the finance council, the council has its primary relationship with him.

14. Membership in the Parish Finance Council

The parish finance council has a narrower and a more technical focus than the pastoral council, hence its membership is smaller in number and more specialized in qualifications.

Though many of its functions are similar to those of other finance committees, for example, at a condominium or country club or not-for-profit enterprise, the vision and purpose of the finance council is that of a parish, a community committed to Christ and his mission in the world, and conscious of the workings of the Holy Spirit. The members of the finance council need to be always aware of this identity and sense of purpose.

The *Code of Canon Law* states that the principal purposes for which the Church possesses temporal goods are: to carry on divine worship, to care for its ministers, and to carry out the works of the apostolate and of charity, especially those for the poor (c. 1254 §2).

Canon Law

The diocesan regulations for finance councils should be consulted at every turn, and especially here on the issue of membership. These regulations or guidelines complement the instructions found in the 1983 *Code of Canon Law*, canon 537, and the corresponding canons on the diocesan finance council (cc. 492 & 493) which can be applied by analogy to parish finance councils.

Catholics. Canon 537 states that the council members should be "Christian faithful," by which it means Catholics who are in full communion with the Church; they should be actively participating members (cf. cc. 96, 204-205; *CCEO* cc.7-8).

Parishioners. The same canon implies, but does not state, that the members should be parishioners, members of the parish. The finance council assists the pastor in the administration of the goods and funds which belong to the parish. It is only fitting that its members should be members of the parish community, and, as a rule, they are. However, it sometimes happens that a person who does not live within the parish boundaries is still considered a parishioner and could be called upon to serve. This would be an exception to the norm of canon 518 (*CCEO* c.

280 §1) which describes parishes in terms of the Catholic faithful within a given territory.

Remember that "the Christian faithful" includes, in addition to lay persons, members of religious communities and even those who are ordained. Hence, a priest, deacon, or religious woman or man, with the suitable skills, could serve on the finance council. Still, the presumption is that the members would usually be lay women or men.

Number

The single canon on parish finance councils does not specify the number of members that should make up a council, but diocesan guidelines often do suggest a number, usually between three and seven persons. Canon 492 §1 calls for the diocesan finance council to have at least three members.

Pastor. The parish finance council is to assist the pastor, hence the pastor is not a member of the council, it is advisory to him. The pastor presides over the council, but someone else may be appointed or elected to chair its meetings; or the chair can be rotating. But, even if the pastor chairs the meetings of the council, he does not have a vote in its proceedings.

The finance council cannot act without a pastor; so at the vacancy of the office of pastor, the finance council ceases to exist. The new pastor appoints a new finance council or confirms the previous council as soon as possible after taking office.

Business Manager. If the parish has an administrator or business officer, that person can be a member of the finance council (unless the diocesan guidelines provide otherwise); but if he or she is a member, it should preferably be as a nonvoting member. The presence of the administrator to the council is important for purposes of communication and resources; but as a voting member, he or she might exercise an exaggerated influence.

Selection and Appointment

Members of the parish finance council are appointed or approved by the pastor, even if preceded by processes of soliciting volunteers, nominations or consultation. Diocesan guidelines may call for a more detailed selection process. Present members of the finance council or of the pastoral council could be asked for suggestions of new members.

The names of the members of the finance council should be made known to the parish community on a regular basis, by listing in the parish bulletin or other means.

Relatives of the pastor by blood or marriage may not serve on the finance council.

The pastor, at his discretion, may remove any member of the council. If a council member resigns, is removed, or dies, the pastor may appoint another member to complete the unexpired term of office.

Terms of Office. Members of the finance council should be appointed for a specific term of office, for example, three or five years, but renewable. Diocesan guidelines may specify the terms of office. Canon 492 §1 states that *diocesan* finance council members are to serve for five-year terms, renewable for more. It seems preferable to stagger the terms of office of council members in the interest of continuity.

Qualifications. The *Code of Canon Law* does not specify any qualifications for membership on the *parish* finance council, but diocesan guidelines probably suggest some; and, obviously, they should be honored as far as possible. The Code does call for the *diocesan* finance council members to be "truly expert in financial affairs and civil law" and "outstanding in integrity" (c. 492 §1). The understanding of a budget process and the ability to read financial balance sheets are important, but so are business and management expertise, and awareness of the law. Finance councils most often include accountants, bankers, attorneys, brokers, and other financial professionals, but they are not limited to those areas of involvement or experience.

Personal honesty, trustworthiness, and a genuine commitment to the welfare of the parish are of paramount importance. Maturity, prudence, and the ability to work collaboratively are also valuable traits.

Conflicts of interest are to be avoided in the appointment of finance council members. For example, those suppliers, contractors, bankers, or accounting firms who do business with the parish should not be placed in a position of overseeing their own business transactions with the parish.

15: OPERATION OF THE PARISH FINANCE COUNCIL

In Chapter Twelve we defined the "function" of the parish finance council as assisting the pastor in the administration of parish goods. In this chapter we will show the "operation" of the finance council. The operation is governed by the Church's universal law, in which finance councils advise the pastor, the parish's official representative in juridic affairs. The finance council operation is also governed by the norms issued by the diocesan bishop. These norms give pastors and councils specific diocesan guidance.

We can anticipate the content of diocesan guidelines by looking at two documents published by the U.S. Conference of Catholic Bishops since 1995. In these documents the bishops have laid out a broad vision for finance councils, and many of the USCCB's recommendations have found their way into diocesan guidelines. The chapter will unfold in two ways. First, we will see how the bishops have recommended a role for the finance council in relation to financial controls and management. The recommendations express the bishops' hopes for finance councils. Second, we will see how actual finance councils have accepted the role recommended by the bishops. We have empirical knowledge of finance councils thanks to a study of councils undertaken in 2007. By comparing what the bishops recommend with the empirical study, we can generalize about the operations of finance councils.

Finance Councils and Financial Controls

In 1995, the U.S. bishops published a booklet entitled *Diocesan Internal Controls: A Framework*. "Internal controls" refers to the system of accounting safeguards that protects the church's assets and produces accurate financial statements. Such controls are useful for all organizations in a diocese, including the parish. In 2010, the recommendations of *Diocesan Internal Controls* were adapted (Zech [2010], 76) for parishes under nine headings:

1. Parishes should be required to adhere to a prescribed budget process, resulting in an annual budget.

2. Periodically parishes should report operating results versus budgeted amounts.

3. Monthly comparative financial statements should be prepared so that appropriate actions could be taken if the actual results vary materially from those budgeted.
4. Parishes should establish policy and procedures manuals to ensure that similar transactions are handled in similar manners.
5. The number of bank accounts should be strictly limited to allow greater control and less opportunity for error or wrongdoing.
6. Authorized check signers should be very limited.
7. Checks in large amounts should require the signature of two responsible individuals.
8. Bank statements should be reconciled by someone other than the check signers.
9. Checks should be drawn according to procedures prescribing adequate supporting documentation.

These are the types of parish internal controls that bishops recommend, not just for the diocese but for the parish as well. Do parishes actually utilize these controls? Are they part of the regular operations of parish finance councils?

Actual Finance Councils

In order to learn how real parish finance councils operate, researchers from Villanova University, the Center for Applied Research in the Apostolate, and the Archdiocese of Philadelphia studied 530 parishes and found that many finance councils actually employ the controls recommended by the U.S. Bishops. The researchers correlated the nine recommendations of the U.S. Bishops with the responses of the 530 parishes.

1. Budgets. Most parishes follow the recommendations of the bishops concerning the budget. For example, "Over 90 percent of the parishes in our sample," said the researchers "prepare an annual operating budget." Furthermore, "Among those that prepare a budget, the parish finance council was involved at some level in all but 2 percent of the parishes" (Zech [2010], 76). At least half of the re-

spondents say that the budget process includes (1) a consultation with parish ministries and (2) the presentation of a draft budget to the parish pastoral council for feedback. Although a few parishes explain their draft budget in the bulletin or at Mass (a process that enhances oversight), nevertheless the majority do not. But at least with regard to the budget, most finance councils are widely involved in budget preparation and follow a prescribed process, just as the bishops have recommended.

2. Actual Spending. The 2007 study also contains good news regarding the examination of actual financial spending in comparison to budgets. At least 80 percent of finance councils review actual versus budgeted amounts at least quarterly (Zech [2010], 79). In this way, the finance council exercises oversight in parishes.

3. Comparisons. Most pastors and finance councils prepare quarterly statements about the relation of budget to actual spending. Such statements enable pastors to take appropriate action should actual results vary significantly from those budgeted. The bishops have recommended monthly reports as the standard, not quarterly reports. Most finance councils do not meet the monthly standard. But at least finance councils regard the comparison of actual amounts to budget amounts as one of their responsibilities.

4. Manuals. Manuals to guide routine transactions ensure that similar transactions are handled in similar manners. The 2007 survey showed that about two-thirds of parishes follow manuals provided by the diocese regarding the responsibilities of the finance council and accounting procedures (Zech [2010], 80). This use is an excellent way of controlling finances. Unfortunately, the studies also showed that one-sixth of parishes do not adhere to a finance council manual or an accounting manual. This is an area in which many finance councils can help to strengthen the parish's dedication to financial controls.

5. Accounts. The 2007 survey shows that more than one-half of parishes have only a single checking account (apart from the parochial school). This testifies to the widespread adoption of financial controls and the limitation of accounts.

Disturbing, however, is the news that more than 40 percent of parishes have more than one checking account, "presumably held by individual parish organizations" (Zech [2010], 80-81). This is a practice that needs to be closely monitored, and the finance council should bring it to the pastor's attention.

6. Signers. The bishops recommend that authorized check signers should be limited. The survey found that the pastor is most frequently authorized to sign checks, and that 1.41 is the average number of authorized check signers per parish (Zech [2010], 82). Limiting the check signers is an effective financial control.

7. Double Signature. The bishops recommend two signers for large disbursements. In 1995, the bishops stated, "Checks in excess of a certain dollar amount (e.g., $1,000) should require the signatures of two responsible individuals" (USCCB [1995], in the section on "Establishing Internal Controls"). While the dollar amount should be adjusted for inflation, the control is an important one. The 2007 survey found that "In two-thirds of the parishes in our sample, only one person was authorized to sign checks, no matter how large the amount" (Zech [2010], 82). Here the finance council can advise the pastor.

8. Reconciliation. In most parishes, bank statements are reconciled by someone other than the check signer. But this is not a universal practice. The survey discovered that in about 9 percent of parishes sampled, "the same person had sole responsibility for both writing checks and reconciling bank statements" (Zech [2010], 84). Sound financial practice calls for the separation of duties.

9. Documentation. The bishops recommend regular procedures for documenting checks. The documentation explains and justifies the expense. 91 percent of parishes indicate that they require this documentation (Zech [2010], 86).

In 1995, when the U.S. Bishops published *Diocesan Financial Controls*, they mainly focused on controls at the diocesan level. But the financial controls recommended for dioceses proved useful at the parish level. The 2007 survey has shown that parishes have actually incorporated many of these controls, often at the urging of finance councils and occasionally under finance council direction. Finance councils apply financial controls principally through their review of the parish budget, and the later comparison of operating results to budgeted amounts. The 2007 survey indicated various other ways in which finance councils advise pastors regarding controls. These provide important clues regarding the operation of the finance council. It operates in part by helping pastors to understand and apply these controls.

Recommended Scope of the Finance Council

If *Diocesan Internal Controls* implied in 1995 a role for finance councils that many finance councils have adopted, the U.S. Bishops' 2009 document *Diocesan Financial Issues* has made the role more explicit. *Diocesan Financial Issues* focuses on the diocese, but it includes a section dedicated explicitly to *parish* financial management. In that section, the bishops lay out 21 "recommended areas for finance council consultation" (USCCB [2009], section I-I, 9-12). The areas for consultation may be divided into seven types:

1. Extraordinary Administration. Acts of extraordinary administration are usually defined by diocesan statutes. Among these acts are large commitments of parish resources which may require diocesan approval. In these cases, the pastor might consult the finance council before seeking approval.

2. Fiscal Management. Pastors may also consult the finance council about the establishment of bank accounts, the preparation of the parish budget, the review of financial reports such as balance sheets, income statements, and bank accounts, the amount of parish indebtedness, and the implementation of diocesan fiscal policy.

3. Reporting. The finance council may advise the pastor about the annual report to the bishop and to the congregation regarding finances, and on reporting requirements if the parish is a civil corporation.

4. Internal Controls. This term refers to the practices by which an organization or parish ensures that its operations and finances will enable it to properly achieve its goals. Internal controls detect errors and safeguard assets. Pastors

may consult the finance council about written procedures for handling cash, reviewing records, and engaging in audits, as well as procedures to prevent conflicts of interest and fraud.

5. Construction. The construction and renovation of facilities, the purchase or lease of property, and the maintenance of buildings are all areas about which the finance council can advise the pastor.

6. Fundraising. The pastor may want to consult the finance council about the effectiveness of fundraising activities, their compliance with civil laws, and the establishment of a parish endowment program.

7. Personnel Matters. The finance council may advise the pastor on hiring, evaluating, and possibly firing a business manager or an employee who provides business services.

These areas of consultation reveal that the finance council has an enormous scope for potential action. The pastor may consult it on virtually any matter having to do with the goods of the parish. But do pastors actually consult finance councils in these areas?

The Scope of Finance Councils in Practice

Published results from a 2007 survey show that most finance councils follow at least some of the bishops' recommendations. For example, the bishops had recommended that pastors consult the finance council about (1) cash receipts and disbursements, (2) unpaid bills, (3) cash on hand, (4) the financial balance sheet, (5) comparisons of actual expenditures and income with budgeted figures, (6) comparisons of current expenditures and income with figures from the previous year, and (7) the amount of outstanding debt. The survey found that in three-fourths of parishes the finance council reviewed these matters at least quarterly (Zech [2010], 66). This testifies to what we already seen: a majority of finance councils involve themselves in fiscal oversight of the budget.

The survey noted, however, that not all of the parishes reviewed each of these items on a quarterly basis. A small percentage of finance council's never reviewed unpaid bills, cash receipts and disbursements, outstanding debts, cash on hand, or balance sheets. Moreover, the survey suggests that there are many opportunities for finance council consultation, especially in the area of financial controls, of which pastors do not avail themselves. They may be missing opportunities to make the parish finances more secure.

The survey also asked parishes about the involvement of the parish finance council is five areas of decision-making:

- Hiring/firing senior parish staff,
- Contracting with outside vendors,
- Consulting about the parish operating budget,
- Developing parish financial policy, and
- Identifying long-range parish financial/physical needs (Zech [2010], 66).

The U.S. Bishops, we recall, had recommended each of these as an area for possible consultation with the finance council. But in the 2007 survey, less than half of the 530 respondents said that the finance council was involved in making these decisions. In some parishes, the finance council was not involved at all. The U.S. bishops have laid out an ambitious finance council agenda, we can say; but most parishes have not yet made it their own.

Leadership, Meetings, Formation

The 2007 study provides us with information about the leadership of parish finance councils, their agenda, the frequency of their meetings, and the formation of council members.

Leadership. Canon 537 does not say that the pastor "presides" over meetings of the finance council. But the presider's role, along with the consultative nature of the finance council, are implicit in the statement that finance councils aid the pastor in the administration of parish goods. He is the parish's legal representative.

The official documents of the church do not spell out what it means for the pastor to preside at meetings. To preside is a function of leadership. It can be exercised unilaterally (for example) by the pastor who sets the agenda, consults, receives recommendations, and decides. It can be exercised collegially (to give another example) by the pastor who builds trust, fosters consensus, leads prayer, and helps the council achieve its ends. Presiding at a council meeting is no single set of behaviors.

But we can distinguish between the one who presides and the one who chairs. The pastor-presider need not be the chairperson of the finance council. The presider may consult without actually running the meeting. That may be left to a chairperson who adheres to the agenda, recognizes speakers, polls the members, and summarizes discussions. In response to the question of who chairs the finance council meeting, the 2007 study (Zech [2010], 65) reported that responses were split "among the pastor (35 percent), a chair elected by the finance council members (34 percent), and an appointed chairperson (26 percent)." Presiders may chair the meeting or may share leadership duties with a separate chairperson.

Meetings. The finance council is a consultative body whose task will vary from meeting to meeting. The agenda depends on the matter about which the pastor most urgently wants advice. But the finance council, like every consultative body, needs to prepare for meetings, and a written agenda can facilitate such preparation. Since the pastor consults the council, he should oversee its agenda, which may be developed in concert with the council chairperson and others.

The 2007 study found that forty percent of finance councils meet monthly, and thirty-four percent meet quarterly. The remainder meets every other month (fifteen percent), twice a year (six percent) or even less frequently (Zech [2010], 64-65). Most respondents indicated that the frequency of meetings is adequate. The frequency of meetings depends on the amount and quality of advice sought by the pastor, as well as on the norms issued by the diocesan bishop. If he is not to exhaust his finance councillors, he must employ them wisely and express his gratitude for their expertise.

Formation. The U.S. Bishops have recommended that parish finance council members be thoroughly trained. They even include an agenda for a finance council training workshop (USCCB [2009], I-I-5). The 2007 study reported, however, a "dearth of education and formation" available to council members (Zech [2010], 67). Even though most finance council members are financial professionals, they may not be aware of the needs of a nonprofit and faith-based organization, or the canon law that governs the church. Such training can help council members to offer the pastor the financial assistance most useful to him.

Summary

The 2007 study has enabled us to ascertain the operation of actual finance councils. It shows that finance councils exercise financial control primarily through the development of the parish budget, in which virtually every finance council is involved. Most finance councils consult with parish ministry groups about the budget and present a draft budget to the parish pastoral council. In addition, most finance councils compare actual spending to budgeted amounts. The work of most finance councils is guided by procedures as defined in published manuals. In these ways, the majority of finance councils exercise financial control.

The bishops have recommended many areas in which pastors may consult their finance councils. The 2007 survey showed that most pastors consult their finance councils about cash receipts and disbursements, about current expenditures in relation to figures from the previous year, and about parish debt. But the data also suggest that there is no fixed manner of consultation, and that some pastors do not consult about these matters at all. In short, we know about the operation of finance councils in the main, but we also know that each finance council is different in its relation to the pastor. The Church is far from following uniform procedures in financial controls and in the operation of finance councils.

Conclusion: Consultation as Collaboration

Parish pastoral and finance councils express Vatican II's teaching on the church as the people of God. As communities of God's people, each living in its own place and time, the church must heed the signs of the times and adapt itself to new circumstances. This calls for the recognition of other gifts, experiences, and points of view in addition to those of the pastors of parishes. Councils harness the power of these other gifts and experiences. In councils, pastors call upon gifted people to share their wisdom about parish leadership and stewardship.

The present book has described, from the standpoint of theology, canon law, and contemporary studies, what councils mean and how they are intended to work. Starting from an analysis of the church's documents, the book has defined councils, shown how the Church has envisioned them, and drawn out the implications of official teaching for relations between pastors and council members. The Church recognizes the gifts of the baptized. Their gifts of practical wisdom, education, and expertise, as well as their life experiences, can enrich the Church. Baptism has incorporated individuals and their gifts within the people of God. Such incorporation carries with it the obligation to serve. It belongs to the mission of gifted people to put their talents at the service of the parish.

Underpinning this reliance upon the gifts of each parishioner is faith in God's Holy Spirit. The Spirit bestows gifts everywhere. Wise pastors recognize this and know how to put these gifts at the service of the community. Every pastor recognizes that his own insights are partial and limited. The prudent pastor reaches out, beyond the parish staff, to gifted members of his community. By consulting them regularly, he invites their participation in his ministry. In so doing, he not only manifests his own pastoral leadership, he also reveals his faith in the Holy Spirit, who animates the community and builds it up.

This implies an aspect of pastoral leadership that, until Vatican II, received far less emphasis than it does today. Pastors have always recognized the importance of consultation since Jesus depicted the good shepherd as the one who knows and listens to the flock. Heightening the importance of consultation in recent years is the growth in the size of congregations and the complexity of synthesizing the views of parishioners. It is relatively easy to hear a few voices and to acknowledge their wisdom. It is far more difficult to listen to a multitude of voices, to discern what is truly wise, and to act on it in a way that will build up the community. Pastoral and finance councils have brought this aspect of pastoral leadership, consultation as collaboration, to the fore.

The recognition of this need will doubtless have consequences for the formation and continuing education of priests. It will also have consequences for parishioners, who have a right to participate in parish life to the best of their abilities.

We can see that Vatican II's teaching about councils has opened up many avenues for further research:

- Priesthood Today. If the effective pastor is the one who knows how to consult, what constitutes a good consultation? About what should a pastor consult? How does the relationship between the pastor and the council members develop over time, as mutual trust and understanding grow?
- Contemporary Parish Life. What distinguishes the parish in which thorough consultation takes place regularly from the parish where it does not? How does consultation enrich the life of the parish? How does it improve decision-making by priests?
- Training in consultation. What do priests need to know in order to consult well? Should training in the arts of consultation change the shape of priestly formation? How can parish members learn to participate more effectively when consulted?

Researching these questions may strengthen pastoral leadership and enable the people of God to put their gifts more fully at the community's service.

By laying the foundation for pastoral and finance councils, Vatican II has expanded our understanding of priestly leadership. Its teaching about councils suggests that pastoral excellence demands more than the ability to teach, preach, and celebrate the sacraments. It includes the ability to build community, and that requires the skills of consultation. Every good pastor helps the congregation to be "one in Christ." The Eucharist is the celebration, the crowning, of that achievement of unity. But pastoral and finance councils contribute to that unity as well. They invite us to deepen our ideas of priestly leadership and of participation by the people of God.

Sources

Acta et Decreta Concilii Planarii Baltimorensis Tertii, 1884. Baltimore: Typis Joannis Murphy, 1886.

Asselin, Anne. "Lay People as 'Protagonists in the Church': Pathways for the Future," *Canon Law Society of America Proceedings* 76 (2014) 119-136.

Beal, John, et al. eds. *New Commentary on the Code of Canon Law*. New York & Mahwah, NJ: Paulist Press, 2000.

Benedict XV. *Codex Iuris Canonici*. June 27, 1917. Romae: Typis PolyglottisVaticanis, 1933.

Borras, Alphonse. *La parrocchia: Dirito canonico e prospettive pastorali*. Bologna: Edizioni Dehoniane, 1997.

Brough, Michael. "Standards for Excellence." In Holmes (ed.), *A Pastor's Toolbox* (2014), pp. 112-123.

Canon Law Digest. Fourteen volumes. Washington, DC: Canon Law Society of America. 1934-2012.

Coccopalmerio, Francesco. *De Paroecia*. Roma: Ed. Pont. Università Gregoriana, 1991.

Congregation for Bishops. "Directory on the Pastoral Ministry of Bishops" *Ecclesiae imago*, May 31, 1973. Ottawa: Publications Service of the Canadian Catholic Conference, 1974.

Congregation for Bishops. "Directory for the Pastoral Ministry of Bishops" *Apostolorum successores*, 2004. Vatican City: Libreria Editrice Vaticana, 2004. Also available at the official Vatican web site, www.vatican.va

Congregation for Clergy. Instruction, *The Priest, Pastor and Leader of the Parish Community*, August 4, 2002. *Origins* 32:23 (November 14, 2002), 374-390.

Congregation for Clergy. "Private Letter on 'Pastoral Councils'" *Omnes Christifideles*, 1973. Published in reference to canon 423 in James I. O'Connor, editor, *The Canon Law Digest*, vol. VII, pp. 280-288.

Congregation for Clergy, et al. Instruction, *Certain Questions Regarding the Cooperation of Lay Faithful in the Ministry of Priests*. *Origins* 27:24 (November 27, 1997) 397-404.

Coriden, James, et al. eds. *The Code of Canon Law: A Text and Commentary*. New York & Mahwah, NJ: Paulist Press, 1985.

Coriden, James, *The Parish in Catholic Tradition: History, Theology and Canon Law*. New York & Mahwah, NJ: Paulist Press, 1997.

Dantuono, Mary Ann. "Legal Principles and Pastoral Issues." In Vincentian Center, *Catholic Church Management* (2010), pp. 201-236.

DeLambo, David, and Richard Krivanka. "Appreciative Inquiry: A Powerful Process for Parish Listening and Planning." Chapter 5 in Fischer and Raley, *Four Ways*, pp. 87-101.

Dogmatic Constitution on the Church. See Vatican II, *Dogmatic Constitution on the Church*.

Fischer, Mark F., and Mary Margaret Raley. *Four Ways to Build More Effective Parish Councils: A Pastoral Approach*. Mystic, CT: Twenty-Third Publications, 2002.

Fischer, Mark. *Pastoral Councils in Today's Catholic Parish*. Mystic, CT: Twenty-Third Publications, 2001.

Fischer, Mark. "What Was Vatican II's Intent Regarding Parish Councils," *Studia Canonica* 33 (1999) 5-25.

Fischer, Mark. *Making Parish Councils Pastoral*. New York & Mahwah, NJ: Paulist Press, 2010.

Francis. *The Joy of the Gospel (Evangelii gaudium)*. Apostolic Exhortation of November 24, 2013. Washington, DC: USCCB, 2013. Also available at the official Vatican web site, www.vatican.va

Griese, Orville. "The New Code of Canon Law and Parish Councils." *Homiletic and Pastoral Review* 85:4 (Jan. 1985) 47-53.

Gubish, Mary Ann, and Susan Jenny, SC, with Arlene McGannon. *Revisioning the Parish Pastoral Council: A Workbook*. New York and Mahwah, NJ: Paulist Press, 2001.

Hermann, Sr. Brenda, MSBT, ACSW and Msgr. James T. Gaston, MA, STL. *Build a Life-Giving Parish: The Gift of Counsel in the Modern World*. Ligouri, MO: Ligouri Publications, 2010.

Hinze, Bradford. *Practices of Dialogue in the Roman Catholic Church: Aims and Obstacles, Lessons and Laments*. New York: Continuum, 2006.

Holmes, Paul A., ed. *A Pastor's Toolbox: Management Skills for Parish Leadership*. Collegeville, MN: Liturgical Press, 2014.

Howes, Robert G. *Creating an Effective Parish Pastoral Council*. Collegeville: The Liturgical Press, 1991.

I beni temporali della Chiesa. Atti del Convegno (Passo della Mendola, 3-7 Iuglio 1995) Quaderni della Mendola 4. Milano: Edizioni Glossa, 1997.

Ippolito, Joseph; Mark Latcovich, and Joyce Malyn-Smith. *In Fulfillment of Their Mission: The Duties and Tasks of a Roman Catholic Priest*. Washington, DC: National Catholic Education Association, 2008.

John Paul II. *Code of Canon Law*, January 25, 1983. Latin-English Edition. Washington, DC: Canon Law Society of America, 1999.

John Paul II. Post-Synodal Apostolic Exhortation, "On the Vocation and the Mission of the Lay Faithful in the Church and in the World" (*Christifideles laici*), December 30, 1988. *Origins* 18:35 (Feb. 9, 1989), 561-595.

John Paul II. *Code of Canons of the Eastern Churches* (October 18, 1990). Latin-English Edition. Washington, DC: Canon Law Society of America, 2001.

John Paul II. Apostolic Exhortation, "Jesus Christ the Saviour and his Mission of Love and Service in Asia" (*Ecclesia in Asia*), January 22, 1999. *Origins* 29 (1999-2000) 357-384.

John Paul II. Apostolic Letter, "At the Beginning of the New Millennium" (*Novo Millennio Ineunte*), January 6, 2001. Boston: Pauline Books and Media, 2003. Available at the official Vatican web site, www.vatican.va

Keating, John. "Consultation in the Parish." *Origins* 14:17 (Oct. 11, 1984): 257, 259-266.

Kennedy, Robert T. "Shared Responsibility in Ecclesial Decision-Making." *Studia Canonica* 14:1 (1980): 5-23.

Kim Se-Mang, Peter. *Parish Councils on Mission: Coresponsibility and Authority among Pastors and Parishioners*. Kuala Lumpur: Benih Publisher, 1991.

La Parrocchia. Studi Giuridici XLIII. Città del Vaticano: Libreria Editrice Vaticana: 1997.

Lundholm-Eades, Jim. "A Six-Month Game Plan." Chapter 3 in Holmes (Editor), *A Pastor's Toolbox* (2014), pp. 31-40.

Lundholm-Eades, Jim. "Parish Planning." Chapter 12 in Holmes (Editor), *A Pastor's Toolbox*, pp. 124-137.

Marzoa, Rodríguez, et al., eds. *Commentario Exégetico al Código de Derecho Canónico*. Eight vols. Pamplona: EUNSA, 1997.

McGovern, John. "Risk Management." Chapter 6 of Holmes (Editor), *Toolbox*, pp. 63-72.

McKenna, Kevin, et al. eds. *Church Finance Handbook*. Washington: Canon Law Society of America, 1999.

McKinney, Mary Benet. *Sharing Wisdom: A Process for Group Decision-Making*. Allen, TX: Tabor Publishing, 1987.

Olsen, Charles. *Transforming Church Boards into Communities of Spiritual Leaders*. New York: The Alban Institute, 1995.

Pagé, Roch. *Les Églises particulières. Tome II*. Montreal: Les Éditions Paulines, 1989.

Paul VI. Apostolic Letter, written *Motu proprio*, on the Implementation of the Decrees *Christus Dominus*, *Presbyterorum Ordinis* and *Perfectae Caritatis* (*Ecclesiae Sanctae*, 6 August 1966). In *Canon Law Digest*, Vol. 6, and in Vatican II, *The Vatican Collection*, Vol. I, pp. 591-610.

Paul VI. Encyclical Letter on "The Paths of the Church" *Ecclesiam suam*, 6 August 1964.

Peri, Paul F. *Catholic Parish Administration: A Handbook*. New York and Mahwah: Paulist Press, 2012.

Pickett, William L. *A Concise Guide to Pastoral Planning*. In the *Concise Guide* series edited by Kevin E. McKenna. Notre Dame, IN: Ave Maria, 2007.

Rademacher, William J. *The Practical Guide for Parish Councils*. West Mystic, CT: Twenty-Third Publications, 1979.

Rademacher, William J., with Marliss Rogers. *The New Practical Guide for Parish Councils*. Mystic, CT: Twenty-Third Publications, 1988.

Renken, John. "Pastoral Councils: Pastoral Planning and Dialogue Among the People of God," *The Jurist* 53 (1993) 132-154.

Renken, John. "Pope Francis and Participative Bodies in the Church: Canonical Reflections," *Studia Canonica* 48:1 (2014) 203-233.

Shaughnessy, Mary Angela. "Parish Administration and Civil Law." Chapter 5 of Zech, editor, *The Parish Management Handbook* (2003), pp. 90-112.

Sweetser, S.J., Thomas P., and Carol Wisniewski Holden. *Leadership in a Successful Parish.* New York, et al., Harper and Row, 1987.

Synod of Bishops. "The Ministerial Priesthood" *De Sacerdotio ministeriali*, Nov. 30, 1971. Reprinted in James I. O'Connor, ed. *The Canon Law Digest*, Vol. VII: *Officially Published Documents Affecting the Code of Canon Law 1968-1972*. Chicago: Chicago Province of the Society of Jesus, 1975.

Tanner, Norman. ed. *Decrees of the Ecumenical Councils.* Vol. II. Washington, DC: Georgetown University Press, 1990.

Thompson, James W. "Stewardship: Financial Control and Accountability." Chapter 12 of Vincentian Center, *Catholic Church Management*, pp. 237-266.

United States Conference of Catholic Bishops, Committee on Budget and Finance. *Diocesan Financial Issues.* Originally published in 2002. Revised edition. Washington, DC: USCCB, 2009. Available at the USCCB website and accessed on Feb. 14, 2015.

United States Conference of Catholic Bishops. *Diocesan Internal Controls: A Framework.* Written by the Committee on Budget and Finance, National Conference of Catholic Bishops. Washington, DC: USCCB, 1995. Also available at the USCCB website and accessed on April 16, 2015.

United States Conference of Catholic Bishops, Ad Hoc Committee on Diocesan Audits, Most Rev. Daniel F. Walsh, Chairman. "Report to the Body of Bishops." Washington, DC: United States Conference of Catholic Bishops, Nov. 12, 2007. Available at the USCCB website and accessed on February 13, 2015.

United States Conference of Catholic Bishops. *Stewardship: A Disciple's Response.* Originally approved by the U.S. Catholic Bishops in 1992. Tenth Anniversary Edition. Washington, DC: United States Conference of Catholic Bishops, 2002. Available at the USCCB website and accessed on Feb. 13, 2015.

Vatican II. *Decree on the Pastoral Office of Bishops in the Church Christus Dominus*, 28 Oct. 1965. In Vatican II, *The Vatican Collection*, Vol. I, pp. 564-590.

Vatican II, *Dogmatic Constitution on the Church Lumen Gentium*, 21 Nov. 1964. In Vatican II, *The Vatican* Collection, Vol. I, pp 350-426.

Vatican II. *The Vatican Collection.* Vol. 1: *The Conciliar and Post Conciliar Documents.* New Revised Edition. General Editor: Austin Flannery, OP. Northport, NY: Costello Publishing Co., 1998.

Vincentian Center for Church and Society, St. John's University, New York. *A Concise Guide to Catholic Church Management.* In the *Concise Guide* Series, Kevin E. McKenna, Series Editor. Notre Dame, IN: Ave Maria Press, 2010.

Wall, Jack. "Pastoring and Administering a Mission-Driven Church." In Holmes (ed.), *A Pastor's Toolbox* (2014), pp. 93-101.

Zech, Charles E., ed. *The Parish Management Handbook.* Mystic, CT: Twenty-Third Publications/Bayard, 2003.

Zech, Charles E., Mary L. Gautier, Robert J. Miller, Mary E. Bendyna. *Best Practices of Catholic Pastoral and Finance Councils.* Huntington, IN: Our Sunday Visitor Publishing Division, 2010.